Moving a Library

by

William H. Kurth
University of California at Los Angeles

and

Ray W. Grim
National Library of Medicine

The Scarecrow Press, Inc.

New York & London   1966

Copyright 1966 by

William H. Kurth and Ray W. Grim

L. C. Card No. 65- 22754

199164

Foreword

When ground was broken for the new building for the National Library of Medicine, in Bethesda, Maryland, in the summer of 1959, the attention of the NLM staff was immediately focused on the problem of moving the collection of more than a million items, which would have to be faced two years hence. Actually, it turned out to be almost three years later when the move was made, and perhaps this extra planning time was one of the factors involved in making the gigantic job go off as smoothly and as efficiently as it did. I have never seen a better executed task in logistics, in or out of the Army.

But more pertinent to the success of the move were the personnel who were assigned the planning responsibility. Ray Grim was then my Executive Officer at NLM, and Bill Kurth was my Deputy Chief of the Reference Division. They pitched in with great energies and came up with detailed plans which in the event turned out to be practically faultless. The major part of the collection had to be moved from downtown Washington, fourteen miles away; a smaller but significant part had to be moved from Cleveland. It was not just a shelf-for-shelf exchange, either; collections which in the old building were broken up because of faulty space arrangements had to be reintegrated, provisions for a new time-segmentation had to be worked out to facilitate the unique and massive NLM photographic interlibrary loan procedures, and, naturally, new allowances of shelf space had to be made for the growing subject-classified and periodical areas. The job was finished in 60 days, in the middle of which period the Library staff offices themselves made the transition, and Library operations were closed down but for a single weekend.

Now Bill and Ray and I have gone our separate ways, far from Bethesda. I salute my old colleagues for that fine job in the Spring of 1962, and for their enterprise in placing the fruits of their experience before the larger library community.

Frank B. Rogers

University of Colorado Medical Center
May 1, 1965

Preface

The authors wish to express their gratitude to Mr. Kenneth Fay and Roy Stricker of the Davidson Transfer and Storage Company, Baltimore, for their part in the National Library of Medicine move, to Joseph McGroarty, Supply Officer of the National Library of Medicine, and the staff of the Reference Services Division for their unremitting attention to this move.

The authors are grateful to the Buildings and Grounds Department, UCLA, especially to Kenneth Pond and King Fitchener who were stalwarts in the move of the UCLA Library collections, June 30 - August 20, 1964, and for the fine cooperation of James Cox and Walter Liebenow and the staff of the Circulation Department of the UCLA Library, who performed magnificently. Appreciation is also due to Paul Miles, Assistant University Librarian, for his help in the course of the UCLA move.

To Dr. Frank B. Rogers, Director of the National Library of Medicine at the time of the move, and to Robert Vosper, University Librarian, University of California, Los Angeles, we owe a special debt.

Contents

Chapter

F I G U R E S

T A B L E S

During 1963-64 we faced a type of task new to most of us at UCLA, that of planning and administering the transfer of some 800,000 volumes from an old library building to the first unit of a new central University Research Library. The task posed some vexing problems. In the first place, it was evident that within the university's academic schedule we could not close down service for more than a long weekend. Thus we had to be in the position of undertaking the move while still providing full-scale public service, including the capacity at any point to provide any particular book for any reader who might request it, with a minimum of delay. Moreover, we were not simply to move a coordinated group of books from one building and replace them in the same arrangement in a new location. The 800,000 volumes to be moved were shelved among a collection of something over a million volumes, and the remaining portions of the collection were to be considered and retained in the old stack for some years to come. Additionally, the old stack had become so crowded that books were lined up on the floors as well as dummied out for shelving in awkward nooks and corners. And of course thousands were charged out to readers so that space had to be projected for their proper return at a later date, in addition to space for the expected growth of the collections over the succeeding few years.

For these several reasons the logistical problem of the move was not a simple one, and I for lack of experience had worried a good deal about it in earlier months. But then good fortune in the guise of the author of this book came onto the scene. I had recently been pleased to bring my old friend William H. Kurth to the UCLA Library as specialist in Latin-American book selection and procurement. But as soon as it was known to us what a superb job he had done just a few months before with the transfer of the National Library of Medicine to its Bethesda quarters, we immediately put him to work, on an overtime basis as it were, as con-

13

sultant to our planning committee dealing with the whole problem of getting into the new building on time and with as little public disability as possible.

The result of his parlayed expertise was a superbly engineered project in which the percentage of error and slippage was almost unnoticeable. Everyone concerned---readers, library staff, and officials of our buildings and grounds department who handled the physical part of the move--were overjoyed with the results of Mr. Kurth's careful planning, foresight, and precision. The present book, in preliminary typescript, was in fact a kind of textbook for us at UCLA, and a mighty good one it was.

Robert Vosper
University Librarian
University of California, Los
   Angeles
February, 1965

Chapter I

Introduction

In treating the subject of moving a library we might regard the moving of a given library as a unique operation, the moving being determined by a set of characteristics describing that library, its size, nature of its services, collection policy, and so forth. We may, however, attempt to isolate the factors which all libraries face in their moving operations; in other words, emphasize the "sameness" or at least determine a common denominator. The purpose of the present work follows the latter concept, that is, to state the factors with which most libraries have to cope.

Thus, the principles recounted are for libraries large as well as small. The present work, in addition, attempts to set out certain methods of operation for the moving process. These methods may be applicable in whole or by adaptation, in part; however, our main effort is to state the broad spectrum of factors involved and to establish--if not the solution--at least suggested channels which might be opportunely utilized.

Basically, the moving operation is a problem in logistics and the correlation of a large number of factors into a coherent, well-functioning plan. Our account, in attempting to set forth and isolate the relevant factors, is in major part based on the practical experience gained in moving the National Library of Medicine (NLM) and its collections of some 1,000,000 items from its old headquarters in Washington, D.C. to its new location in Bethesda, in Maryland (in addition to the moving of 35,000 volumes of rare books in the History of Medicine Division, Cleveland, Ohio, to Bethesda), March-May 1962. In addition, one of the authors was responsible for the planning and direction of the Library of the University of California at Los Angeles move in June-August 1964, a major operation involving some 800,000 volumes (and the shifting of some 100,000 others in the old building). The UCLA move used

15

the methodology set forth in the present text; further, the UCLA
move brought to fruition a number of additional factors peculiar to
"open stack" libraries and the text has been amended appropriately;
statistical by-products of the UCLA Library move, of interest to
the university library community, are also recited.

The authors have attempted to translate experience into principles and procedures which, it is hoped, can be of assistance to
various kinds of libraries engaged in move planning; this has been
preferred to setting down the results of the move in reportorial
style. The text is built rather solidly, we feel, on tried and tested
methods and procedures. There is considerable statistical data,
much of it involved in the process of taking measurements and in
calculating the future need for shelf space.

In a valid sense we may speak of a "series of moves" rather
than a move. This brings into focus what we feel is the objective of
a well-executed move, namely, an orderly, systematic transition
from the existing building to the new library building, so designed
and planned as to cause minimal disruption to the regular operations
of the library. Rapidity of moving, per se, is not the major element though it is directly involved in certain stages of the moving
process. A subsidiary use of the moving operation may be cited:
this is to accommodate changes in the organization or arrangement
of the collections in the new building (either to meet a change in
the library's program or to improve its service). The opportunity
for this exists in the moving operation and by careful analysis and
survey of the relevant factors, can be accomplished such that its effect on the services during "move time" is minimal.

Basic to the successful operation of a move is a thorough understanding of the library's program, its services, the demands upon
those services, and the aggregate of problems requiring solution in
the new building. We have addressed ourselves to a statement of
the wide range of factors which we believe to be of common concern and have stated some of the possible avenues of approach, cit-
ing the techniques and procedures used in the NLM and UCLA move
by way of illustration. We have also, provided some of the tools
for analysis of the individual library moving problem. This, we

believe, is the point at which the individual library difference can
appropriately come into the picture. Again, our approach is in
terms of move factors all libraries, large libraries as well as
small libraries, have to consider.

The scope of the present work can be outlined at this juncture.
It can be said that planning the move starts with designing of the
new building, on the grounds that in the design there are incorporated, implicity or explicitly, the satisfaction of the library's
needs relating to the size, growth, and future development. These
factors, then, would be "built into" the new building. The present
work, however, begins with the existence of a new building (or at
blue print stage) but in any case as fait accompli, regardless of
the "built in" features designed to handle the library's future development. To go beyond this point in the present book involves
building planning, and while some of the aspects of building planning are legitimate concerns of a moving operation broadly con-
ceived, we propose to treat moving only in the present work. We,
therefore, consider the subject of moving with the new building as
a completed entity, of a certain size, expansion possibilities and
physical characteristics. Our "inherited" new building has a deter-
minate set of functions, e.g., a certain number of floors, book
shelves, a set number of square feet of floor space, number of
elevators, exits, etc. These existing factors become essential
bases for purposeful planning of the move.

This states the beginning point of the present work. The end
point is the completed moving of staff, the collections, and the
furniture and equipment into the new building to assure optimum
inter-relationships and with respect to the book collections, the
best possible arrangements to meet the challenging needs of the
future for the given library.

What lies between these two points is the subject matter of the
present work: what the considerations are, how to observe, how to
study, measure, how to establish the administrative structure for
the move and how to take into account the myriad factors involved.

The presentation has been simplified by having a "glossary of
terms" (in the appendix) since it has been necessary to use a spe-

cial "jargon" or to use terminology of special form.

Chapter II

Preview Of The Library Move And The Administrative Aspects

Purpose

The purpose of the present chapter is to sketch and outline the entire panorama of factors involved in the moving of a library, as a prelude to the more detailed and extensive treatment these factors receive in the following chapters.

The presentation here is designed for the library's management; accordingly, the administrative aspects are tied into the review of the factors covered in a move.

The considerations outlined

One of the very first considerations of the move planning is the review by the director of libraries or his deputy, of the entire change of items likely to be encountered in the move. Early nomination of the staff member who will be entrusted with the responsibility for the move planning and the direction of the move is essential. The staff member so designated ought to meet a number of requirements. Obviously, he should be thoroughly familiar with the entire library, should understand its program, the work of the various departments, and its services. He ought, further, to know the physical characteristics of the present building and the new building. He should be skilled in shaping complex and interrelated details into a coherent whole and able to give firm direction to the moving operations. Aside from the necessity for submitting periodic reports on the status of the move planning, the move director should be given wide latitude for planning.

In viewing the panorama of move "facts" or potential move events, we have to give consideration to the present building occupied by the library. By this is meant noting the characteristics of the building, its place in the total library environment before, during, and after the move operation has been concluded. Involved,

19

also, is consideration of the furniture and equipment on hand; the disposition or allocation of furniture and equipment located in the present building has to be considered fairly early in the move planning. A systematic "housecleaning," for example, calculated to divest the present building of unneeded furniture, equipment and supplies should be initiated to preclude unnecessary and expensive moving of such material to the new building. This is an essential condition to the later precise inventory of furniture and equipment to be transferred to the new building, which involves the designation of these items for delivery to precise parts of the new building. Study of the present building from the standpoint of possible move routes, the nature and number of exits, location of loading platforms, and need for supplementary exits also cover important areas of planning.

The collections of library materials in the present building may be considered separately and later correlated with the total plan. Here we are concerned with the size of the various collections, their special characteristics, the rationale of arrangement, special forms of material (e.g., oversize books, maps, charts, microfilms, photographs, etc.) The rate of growth sustained by the various collections will be an important ingredient in our later development of the amount of space to be provided in the new bookstacks. These considerations ought to encompass questions relating to the basic arrangement of the collections: Will the organization of the collections be the same as at present? (Can the moving operation be made to contrive a more desirable arrangement of the collections?) Are parts of certain collections in storage or in buildings separate from the main library? Should any existing collections be segmented, or merged? A moving operation, in effect, offers a prime opportunity for the correction of undesirable arrangements which may have evolved over the years due to the lack of space. Basically, the concern put forward here is measurement, observation, and analysis of the existing collections regarding their optimum organization. Should time be available, studies of the use of the collection may be desirable to assist in the accurate description of the separate collections.

The status of the new building will have to be closely examined and its probable completion date predicted and later in the planning, precisely decided upon. The range of factors here covers such elements as the outfitting of the new building with new furniture and equipment. In reality, this constitutes a separate "move"--from the several suppliers directly to the new building and requiring close monitoring and control by the move director to assure conformance of the material to specification and adherence to delivery target dates. Factors such as the fabrication and installation of the cabinets and trays to house the public card catalog and the installation of the electrical system and telephone lines (and designation of the location of instruments), as well as the program of work on the air-conditioning system also must be carefully checked to ascertain that these matters are completed according to schedule. The preparation of a timetable listing the status and progress of such work, as well as furniture and equipment deliveries, is essential because of the necessity, later in the course of the planning, to make a precise determination of the date on which the new library building will become the functioning center of library activities. Around the determination of this date will be fitted the various moving operations, some occurring before this date and others after it.

Study of the new building from the standpoint of logical and efficient move routes from the point of entry and within the new building, taking into account the loading platform, elevators, and aisles is also indicated. These considerations are basic to the movement of the used furniture and equipment to be transferred to the new building and with respect, of course, to the moving of library materials.

The collections of library materials vis à vis the new building represent a separate area of planning to be scheduled, however, for correlation with the total move planning. Here we are concerned with the detailed examination and measurement of the bookstacks, namely, their capacity, the labelling of the various clusters of bookstacks according to a logical plan, their extent according to floors or levels, and their location in terms of elevator, booklift, and stairway access. The arrangement or organization of the

collections of library materials in the new bookstacks, the order or
sequence of shelving to be adopted, which collections should be
shelved in a given area--and the principles we might utilize to decide this--represent other areas we shall have to consider. Further,
the amount of growth space which is available, what growth space
is required for a given collection--and the criteria we might use to
accomplish this--are factors which will have to be weighed. The
study of the new building with respect to the routes to be followed
in moving the collections to their area of placement will also have
to be studied carefully, taking into account the location of the loading platform and the elevators since these are some of the time
and cost factors.

The actual moving of the library, comprising the furniture and
equipment as well as the collections of library materials, invites
attention to a broad range of factors. Who will do the actual moving may serve to introduce the considerations involved. Here
thought has to be given to the manpower factor (together with other
related factors which exert considerable influence: size of the library, availability of library staff, probable duration of the move,
and others). Will the job be executed by the regular library staff?
There exists a constituted staff; it is in being an administrative
entity, and use of library staff would provide the necessary reas-
surance with respect to safeguarding and proper control of the library collections during the actual move operation. On the other
hand, the use of outside help by contract for the execution of the
move may be a logical choice. Outside help can signify two alternatives; professional mover or local manpower within the administrative unit of which the library is a part, e.g., the buildings
and grounds department of a university. The latter has the advantage of permitting the library staff to conduct regular library operations. We may well wish to adopt a combination of these two methods, capitalizing on their advantages and minimizing their disadvantages.

How the library collections will be moved, or the nature of the
techniques to be utilized, represents a factor to be taken into account. This is important for early consideration because, in addi-

tion to determining the methodology, there will be need to imple-
ment the course of action decided upon. If the collections of library materials are to be transferred to the new building in packing boxes, there will be need to determine the quantity, style, and
dimension of the boxes, as well as the planning to describe accurately and precisely how the boxes will be used within the system
(who will pack, how the boxes will be transported, unloaded, etc.)
If booktrucks are to be used (or equivalents of booktrucks) the
mobilization of a sufficient number should be planned. The question of technique also relates to the manner in which the packing
boxes or booktrucks will be conveyed from the present to the new
building. Will the collections of library materials be cleaned during the move operation, or will this be accomplished while the
collections are housed in the present building? The security of the
collections, that is, their safeguarding from damage or loss during
the actual moving is a factor to be considered. The possibility of
inclement weather must also be taken into account. Special pre-
cautionary measures are, of course, particularly important with respect to the rare book materials. The question of adequate safeguards, to minimize damage or loss, is most important; the aspect
of insuring the collections while in transit is another question which
is implicit here. The matter of fumigation to avoid transfer of insect pests to the new building, should have careful attention.

At what point in time the moving operation will be initiated is
an item which is in large measure determined by the readiness of
the new building. Readiness may well have legal implications. The
building will, in all probability, have to be formally accepted by
the administrative agency of which the Library is a part. In addition to the matter of acceptance, there is the outfitting of the new
building which has decisive influence controlling the time when the
move can be initiated. (The installation of the public card catalog,
bookshelves, installation of furniture and equipment, etc. are
examples). The date for the beginning of the move will have to
be set well in advance, as will the date for staff occupancy of the
new building. This will, in most instances, have to be done in ex-

pectation of acceptance and of the completion of the outfitting at a
certain point in time.

The start of moving will also depend on the state of planning
and there will be need for some margin in setting the optimum
time for the execution of the move. Other intangible factors may
be present among which we may cite the need or desire to have
the new building serve as the center of library operations, or to
begin functioning along the lines already set out by the library
administration. The appropriate time, assuming there is some degree of choice in the matter, is contingent, in part, upon the type
of library involved and other things being equal, the choice of a
low-service period would be desirable. For a college or university
library, a vacation period when the service demands upon the library are not as high as they would be during the regular semester, would be appropriate. For a public library, or a library where
service loads may be established at approximately the same level
throughout the year, the area of choice may be more limited. However, the major determinants of when the move will be initiated
are prime readiness of the overall plans, the readiness of the new
building, and the library's requirements for occupying the new building. Freedom of choice of time within these parameters may be
negligible or non-existent.

The duration of the moving operation is partly governed by
choice, but for the most part it is predetermined by the size of
the library collections, the type and extent of the equipment to be
utilized, the nature and size of the manpower (outside personnel as
well as library staff) which will be invested, and the number of
hours which will be devoted by the staff on a day-to-day basis.
These are the factors that will shape and decide the duration of the
move operation. To a certain degree such factors can be managed
so that the total duration of the move is contracted, that is, we
may increase the manpower, increase its daily hours, invest in additional moving equipment, etc. However, the rate of increase,
with the additional inputs of this sort will often not bring about a
proportional increase in productivity, for reasons to be discussed

at a later point.

As a matter of fact, the acceleration of the move may not always be desirable. Relative speed is a by-product of the procedures established, based on reasonable and considered estimates of manpower, equipment, and funds. The objective of the move can be stated to be the efficient transferral of the library to the new building with the least interruption of regular library activities; the duration of the move is a factor which, in very large measure, is determined by these considerations. It should be mentioned, too, that any acceleration of the move process above our original inputs of manpower and equipment, etc. usually can be quite expensive. Moreover, the extra demands upon staff and the hazards due to the increased pace of physical exertion (present even if staff members do not participate in the actual loading and unloading of books) are definitely factors to be given serious attention. A relatively drawn-out moving operation, on the other hand, can be conjoined with adequate library service, meeting our goal. The conservation of the staff, and their well being, represent a corollary to this. Extra demands can usually be met but a price must be paid; in addition, we must give thought to regular library operations following the move and the necessity to have the staff in adequate physical and mental state to meet the new challenge to service which a new building normally provides.

Administration of the Move

The issues presented in outline form will require careful planning and scheduling in order to ensure their execution at the appropriate time. Thus, it is necessary to establish an administrative staff to provide the necessary direction.

The move director will wish to draw together a staff, either full-time or part-time, contingent upon the size and complexity of the move. The specification of their responsibilities to the move director should be carefully outlined to cover the various plans, studies and operations which will have to be consummated. Again, depending on the nature and extent of the move concerned, the move director may wish to consider the establishment of a move

committee, made up of representatives from all the departments
of the library. The function of the move committee would be to advise the move director and his immediate staff, to consider the
ramifications of the move plans upon their department, and to sug-
gest ways and means of performing specific planning and operational tasks. Because the move is a series of inter-related moves, representation from all departments should help to foresee faults in the
planning. Further, individual members of the move committee may
be assigned specific work tasks in connection with the planning as
it relates to their given departments.

The utility of this sort of committee to the move director can
be substantial; he will be concerned, on a daily basis, and even
hourly basis shortly before and during the move, with a voluminous
amount of detail. These matters will run the gamut of the regular
library operations (which will have to go on) and the planning and
operational details of the moving per se. These details will have to
be coordinated and directed by the move director. It is accordingly
essential that the move director prepare as early as possible a
provisional schedule of what will be involved, organize a move
committee, and have it meet to discuss the library's provisional
move plans.

It is well to define the respective functions of the move director and the move committee. The move committee's job is in the
area of weighing plans, suggesting, offering possible alternatives,
working on specific move-connected assignments and in imparting
information to their respective staffs; the final decision-making
ought to be in the hands of the move director, including the establishment of the time schedule and the formulation of the master
move plan.

One responsibility of the move director and his immediate staff
is to provide the director of libraries with a series of status reports on the planning. This sort of reporting can well take the
form of having a presentation of move planning by the move director for the director of libraries and the principal officers, i.e.,
heads of departments of the library. These meetings may be few in

number but are administratively desirable for apprising the key
officials of the library as to the state of the planning. The discussion of particular aspects of the planning may be directed to important factors which should be taken into account.

The move director will be involved in planning and also in the
implementation of plans; thus, a program of checks and re-checks
should be instituted at the beginning of the planning by the move
director to assure that planned work is actually accomplished on
schedule.

Early in the move planning a central move planning office
should be designated. This should be equipped with floor layouts
of the present and new buildings, and as information is gathered
on the various essential move factors they should be conveniently
arranged in such an office. Such planning aids as Chart-Pak,
Boardmaster, etc. should be conveniently available, together with
calculating machine. Suitable provision for staff conferences of the
move committee should be made.

Lines of communication should be established between the move
director and other planning officials or persons involved in the
move, e.g., the architect, construction engineer, and other persons
as the individual move will decide; this may be the university buildings and grounds department. Periodic meetings with such persons
to review the status of the new building construction and to confer
on other essential factors should be held.

It will be necessary to set down, even in very provisional form,
a tentative plan covering the varied elements cited above. This sort
of plan can be desirably arranged in the form of stages or phases
which the entire moving operation will consume. It should be augmented by the addition of preliminary target dates to accomplish
designated stages of the operation. This is definitely a "trial" or
hypothetical statement of intention; its purpose is to outline what
has to be done, allocate the time margin deemed necessary for the
particular operations cited. This is warranted in order to assay
the practicability in terms of time and manpower. This provisional
statement can be criticized, and rearranged as more adequate data

and findings are brought into focus; however, the advantage of making this "trial" plan is to ascertain which factors correlate nicely,
and which ones are non-correlated, i.e., specific operations which
do overlap, and which in practice cannot be permitted to overlap.
Some of the stages recited may be difficult, if not impossible, to
set out in terms of manpower and time requirements, but at this time
our main intention is to record such operations and approximate the
dates by which we estimate their completion in order to examine
the move plan as a whole and to provide a test of its practicability.

Information for the staff

Approximately, a year before the target date for occupancy of
the new building, a program should be instituted to acquaint the
staff with management plans with respect to the new building. This
is most important if the move is to another commuting area and
travel time to and from work affects the majority of staff.

As the new building takes form, the staff will be afforded opportunity to have the building plans explained. The physical characteristics of the new building will be described in sufficient detail
to permit each staff member an understanding of what his new work
environment will be like. New methods, techniques and technological
improvements to be introduced in the new setting will be covered.
New equipment ought to be delivered to the present building when-
ever possible, prior to the move, to allow for familiarization train-
ing for the operators. (For example, the Xerox continuous printer
and mobile microfilm cameras were introduced into routine work
processes at NLM before the move.) Every effort must be made to
lessen the impact of the move on the personal life of the employee.
Surveys should be conducted to determine which employees definitely will not accompany the library to its new location. Those so
choosing will have to be replaced and the replacements trained.
Also, those who choose not to move with the library should be
given every possible assistance for placement in their preferred
location. It should be noted that all of this dislocation of staff
places considerable strain on the work effort, and management
must be prepared to exert extraordinary effort to maintain satis-

factory levels of work production during this period.

More often than not, the transportation problem, if the move of the library implies change to a relatively distant location, governs the employee's decision to stay or leave. Therefore, this item calls for serious attention on the part of management to the possibilities for arranging for car pools; likewise, the library must thoroughly acquaint staff with public transportation schedules, rates and facilities, and provide clearing house information on housing accommodations adjacent to the new site of operations.

The social, cultural and recreational facilities available at or near the new location should be investigated and the facts presented to the staff. Quite often the presence or absence of such facilities could prove to be a decisive factor in the retention or loss of employees.

Once construction has reached a stage of completion where it is safe and practicable to do so, the staff should be given a tour of the new facility.

Although the effect of a move on staff may vary in each instance, common to every case is the truism that our staff is our most important resource. Always of prime importance, it will require more time and attention as moving day draws near.

We are now in a position to discuss some of the factors enumerated in greater detail. This discussion will be by specific topic; however, the planning and associated work projects will, more times than not, be carried out concurrently. These topics, treated separately, are inter-related and will have to be considered in the light of the complete move plan and entered into the master move plan as information is developed. Our discussion, however, treats these topics, by necessity, as discrete items. In Chapter V, we attempt to gather these topics together by discussing the elaboration of the master move plan.

Chapter III

The Present Building Environment

Purpose

The purpose of this chapter is to describe and analyze the present building or, more accurately, the "present building environment." First, the present building is examined from the standpoint of a physical structure--its design, location of various offices, reading rooms, bookstacks, elevators, etc., and the implications these will have on the move operation. Second, the present building is examined with reference to the equipment and furniture used by the various departments in that building for the purpose of transacting their regular operations. Third, the collections of library materials (books, periodicals, maps, microfilms, etc.) are studied. Finally, the present building is examined from the standpoint of interrelationships of the day-to-day work operations among the several departments. These represent the considerations which, in one way or another, are involved in the move planning and in the move operation.

The physical structure of the building plays an important part in the relative ease with which a move operation can proceed. The quantity and nature of the furniture and equipment, also, represent important factors in charting the move plan. The inter-relationships between the departments will have to be taken into consideration in determining the priority of moving the departments (together with their furniture and equipment). The collections of library materials represent the major element in the move and their importance in move planning is evident, for this reason the larger part of the discussion in this chapter concerns collections of library materials. Nevertheless, the moving of the book collections will be affected by the nature of the physical structure of the present building, and, to some extent, the moving of the several departments may have to

30

be correlated with the moving of certain portions of the collections
of library materials.

The present chapter is concerned with the existing state of the
collections of library materials, their location in the present building, their measurement in terms of an adequate and usable unit of
measurement (linear feet). We shall be concerned with developing
the nature and extent of the growth of the various collections since
we shall, be concerned with making suitable provision for this
growth. We will wish to discuss, also, the special forms of library material, identifying them, their location and magnitude,
noting any special procedures which will be necessary to assure
their adequate handling during the moving. A certain collection
may have been split up during past years because of over-crowding
in the present building; here we will wish to determine where these
parts of individual collections are housed and their separate and aggregate size. We may also wish to examine materials which constitute an individual collection from the standpoint of the need for
segmenting such a collection. (This might be on the basis of a
time period, or other distinction considered appropriate.) Implicit
in such labors should be the thought of possible improvement in
the arrangement of the individual collections in the new building;
in other words, we should not wish to be concerned with the move
per se of the individual collections, but should give attention to
possible alternatives which may represent an improvement.

Description of the present library building

It is well to have in hand a good drawing or chart of the present building which illustrates the various rooms, offices, etc.,
labelled as to their present work function. Such a drawing will be
of value in noting exactly what the various rooms and parts of the
building contain and will complement a precise physical inventory of
the present building. The move director and his staff will, of
course, have to familiarize themselves thoroughly with the new
building environment. A full-scale examination of the building is
necessary, to make a determination of the (non-book) material on
hand. Although seemingly trite, it is something amazing what re-

cently explored parts of an old building can yield.

Notation should be made of the number of elevators and their capacity in terms of size and weight. It is important to check the dates of their most recent overhaul and test. The corridors and their relative advantages for the moving of books and furniture and equipment have to be studied. The nature and extent of traffic --staff members and library users--will have to be considered here, and plans made to establish a line of march for the move. Any special hazards, potential accidents, bottlenecks should be noted. Any over-size furniture or equipment should be spotted so that any special moving arrangements may be known well in advance.

The number and location of stairways should be ascertained, and notation made as to their use in the move should elevator service be unavailable for access to certain book collections or equipment. Stairways will bear study, as well, for library staff traffic in the event elevator service has to be coordinated with moving the book collections.

Which particular route or routes within the present building offers the best choice during the moving operation, taking into account the furniture and equipment to be moved to the new building, warrants careful study. For some equipment there may be need for the use of an outside portable elevator (or crane) fitted against a window. If a professional moving concern or other outside assistance is to be involved in the moving of furniture and equipment it is well to have their representatives present for a detailed tour of the present building. Equipment, such as punch-card machinery, flexowriters, photoduplication equipment, will likely require special servicing by the manufacturer just prior to moving to make it ready for the mover. The various pieces of equipment requiring such attention should be noted. The reverse operation of making the equipment ready in the new building will also have to be scheduled.

The present building should be surveyed from the standpoint of priority of move operations. It may be desirable, for example, to move a certain collection in advance of another; however, the location of the preferred collection may be such that a non-preferred

collection must be moved first. Without attempting, at this stage
in the survey of the present building, to make any final determination of the priorities within the move, it is very desirable to examine the collections from this standpoint. An example may be
cited: in the old National Library of Medicine building, the collection of Documents (W-1) encompassing some 3,000 linear feet of
material could ideally have been moved out fairly early in the move
because of moderate use made of this collection. However, in order
to move it considerable traffic would have been entailed--directly
through the work area of the Bibliographic Services Division. This
would have been necessary in order to gain access to the portable
outside elevator which had to be placed against an outside window
next to the Bibliographic Services Division to accommodate the removal of data processing equipment. Thus, the Bibliographic Services Division had to be moved in advance of the Document Collection.

The size of the library collection and the extent of the labor
force will dictate whether there is need for considering a second
or additional exit. A single exit, with its loading platform, may be
sufficient. Consideration will, however, have to be given to the traffic or load this one exit will bear. For a relatively small move it
may be adequate, even for handling furniture and equipment. However, when the move is a major one, a second exit may be very
desirable to provide for greater feasibility and for concurrent moving. The second exit becomes an important consideration when concurrent moving is involved, that is, if two collections are being
moved from the shelves in the present building at the same time. A
second exit which may be utilized can increase production and
avoid the potential bottleneck inherent in a single exit. Of course,
a single exit with its loading platform can be managed by scheduling the pulling of books from two collections simultaneously in such
a way as to stagger their arrival through the single exit to the
loading platform with minor disruption. Yet, a second exit, if it
can conveniently be created, will avoid the necessity for such
planning. A second exit may take the form of removal of a window

on the ground floor, and with the aid of ramps, creating a second
loading platform. It may, alternatively, involve the use of a portable outside elevator such as that used in the National Library of
Medicine move. A portable outside elevator would not, however,
be desirable from the cost standpoint for a relatively small collection.

The present building will require study to ascertain which
auxiliary second exit seems most practicable.

Survey of present furniture and equipment

An important consideration is the question of disposition of the
furniture and equipment which will not be moved to the new building. A good deal of such furniture and equipment will probably
have to be retained for use of the staff up until move time, but
it is important to plan the disposition of such items well in advance
in accordance with a good schedule. Much depends here on the plans
for the present building after the completion of the move to the new
building. Periodic inspections were made by the Property Office at
the National Library of Medicine at frequent intervals in the twelve
month period preceding the move. Much material, in fact several
van loads, were surveyed and disposed of through regular excess
property channels. Yet, despite full cooperation of all department
heads, it was necessary to route to a temporary holding area in
the new building, during the move operation, many items which
could have been disposed of at the old building. The furniture and
equipment which will not be transferred to the new building may be
viewed in a two-fold perspective: that which is not in present use
and can conveniently be re-apportioned to other uses (other agencies, other campus libraries, etc.) and that which will have to be
in use up until move time. With respect to the former category a
disposition schedule should be established to provide for the orderly retirement of such furniture and equipment several months before move time. The latter category is subject to future plans for
the present building--it may be that the furniture and equipment can
merely be left in place depending on future use; on the other hand,
if it will be disposed of by removal to other campus offices or

agencies, it may be desirable to have such furniture and equipment
moved to a central room, tying such operation into the move plan
to avoid interference with the traffic generated by the main move
of book and non-book materials to the new building. The designation of furniture and equipment may be conveniently systematized
by tagging the furniture and equipment into two categories: the material which can be disposed of months ahead of move time, the
material which will be disposed of at move time or shortly thereafter.

The designation and coding of furniture and equipment which
will not be moved to the new building should be given attention. If
the furniture and equipment not being moved to the new building
will remain in place it may not be necessary to code or mark any
of it.

If furniture and equipment is to be removed from the building,
rather than left in the present building, then it ought to be marked.
The deadline for the processing of furniture or equipment should
be specified in the master move plan; indication should be made
as to who will remove the material and at what time. This is all
part of a survey of the furniture and equipment; a product of this
survey will be the identification of furniture and equipment to be
transferred to the new building. This should be listed and notation
made as to the location of the furniture and equipment in the new
building. A specimen page of an inventory of this sort appears as
Figure 1 below. The furniture and equipment so designated for reuse in the new building can be color-coded with the floor (and
room number) marked thereon. Needless to say, inviolate instructions ought to be issued against the removal of such stickers. A
number of logical designations are possible; for example, different
colors can symbolize different floor levels, again bearing the
room number of destination. This type of recording and designation
will simplify the planning and will also be an important help to the
mover in making an accurate and efficient transfer of the equipment and furniture.

Figure 1

Inventory of furniture and equipment to be moved to the new
building

Property number	Description	Present location	Location new bldg.	Remarks
1723	Base, card file, steel height 19", depth 17", width 33"	118	A-50	
1724	Cabinet, card size, 3 3 x 5", steel, 6 drs. wide, 3 drs. high.	118	A-50	
102	Cabinet, steel, up-right, olive green finish, 4 drs. high, 1 dr. wide.	116	A-50	
101	"	116	A-50	refinish
498	Camera, Microfile Recordak Model E.	119	A-50	
2124	Cutter, paper, hand operated, 16" (Premier)	119	A-50	

The careful preparation of an inventory of this sort will pay
large dividends. It will help ensure against overlooking furniture
and equipment which is to be moved. The inventory constitutes a
convenient central record of all furniture and equipment to be moved.
Since it can be organized by division or department of the Library,
it is a ready reference document as to what goes to the new building. The estimation of costs in terms of manpower and moving
equipment is facilitated by such a listing. The list of furniture and
equipment may be useful in meeting administrative requirements;
it may be necessary, for example, to have a list of furniture and
equipment to be moved together with the property number of each
piece. Thus, the careful consideration of the inventory and its possible use is an important step in the move planning. In the course
of grading furniture and equipment for reuse, it should be established well before moving day exactly where the material is to be
assigned in the new building. Decals showing the new building room

location can be applied at this juncture. Chart Pak (Leeds, Massachusetts) makes such decals illustrating desks, files, etc., which can be applied, to scale, on to the drawings of the new floor layouts.

Housecleaning prior to the move

All libraries must undergo periodic housecleaning drives. Considering the perennial insistence of management on the subject and the acute space shortage in library buildings, it would seem that such built-in pressures would operate against the accumulation of an untoward amount of "non-essential" material.

The housecleaning may be viewed separately from the furniture and equipment survey or considered an integral part of it; actually, both have the same objective: to eliminate non-essential materials from the Library on a planned basis to make the move operation function more efficiently. The housecleaning schedule can be combined with the survey of furniture and equipment. The main items to be mentioned in connection with housecleaning consist of records and supply items.

Such a survey can be accomplished on a divisional or departmental basis, under the control of the move director. The survey should be conducted according to a schedule, preferably quite early in the move planning inasmuch as the questions of records disposal, especially, may involve considerable planning. A set of controls will, of course, have to be established to ensure against the discarding of important records or supplies, and the move director should assure himself that adequate safeguards exist by assigning competent personnel to this job.

Insect and rodent infestation

A careful check should be instituted to ascertain the incidence of insect and rodent infestation in the present building. This examination should be conducted by an entomologist or sanitary engineer, and if remedial action is required, the plans will have to be drawn up and fitted in the move plan. It should be stressed that the remedial procedures should be carried out by trained personnel, e.g., local pest control firm with experienced and qualified personnel. It is essential that the book materials moved into the new building be free from infestation.

Preliminary procedures in the measurement of books

We may have on hand a fairly good idea of the magnitude of the individual collections of library materials. Usually the annual report statistics will indicate so many monographic volumes, so many volumes of serials, total reels of microfilms, number of maps, etc. Can we not use the number of volumes reported for an individual collection as a basis for measurement? There are a number of limitations to such a practice. Our measurement is in reality the calculation of shelf displacement, that is, how much shelf space is used by books.

First, volumes differ substantially in width and the standard of "volume" is too variable for purposes of measurement in the context of shelf displacement.[1] Secondly, the library statistics which report volumes on hand may not be consistent in the application of the definition of "volume"; in addition, the increments (and withdrawals) over a long period raise the need for a new count. There may be unbound materials on the shelves which, although not characterized as volumes, nevertheless do take up shelf space. What takes up shelf space, and how much is our major concern.

From the standpoint of a relatively accurate measurement, to describe the magnitude of the individual collections at the present time in terms of the amount of shelf space displaced we introduce an alternative standard of measurement: this is the concept of the linear foot, that is, the number of linear feet of book materials on the shelves or the number of linear feet of shelf space displaced by books on the shelves. "Displacement" here means simply books on the shelf under compression from a bookend.

One immediate possibility in determining the extent of the individual collections, making use of the concept of the linear foot, would be to determine the average number of volumes contained in a linear foot for an individual collection and divide this figure into the total number of volumes reported for that collection. The basic difficulty here is that, aside from the disparity in number of vol-

umes per linear foot--we may secure from 6 volumes per foot up
to 25 or more per linear foot--the reported volume count may not
be accurate enough to give a measurement of shelf displacement,
for the reasons cited above.

   We could, of course, measure each of the individual collections on a shelf-by-shelf basis, that is, we could total up the
linear inches or feet of book materials on each shelf and secure
the necessary figures. While this would provide the desired result,
it would be an arduous job and it would be subject to error, especially in a relatively large collection since the chance of error is
increased when a large number of measurements is involved. The
enormous number of shelves which would require checking on a
shelf-by-shelf examination would make this procedure costly and
time consuming. The fact that the shelves are all, or almost all,
of standard dimensions is a further consideration which invites
sampling. It is desirable, therefore, to think in terms of sampling.

   As pointed out by W. Allen Wallis and Harry V. Roberts in Statistics; A New Approach. (Glencoe, Ill., The Free Press of Glencoe, 1956). p. 112.

> Even where complete inspection is possible, sampling may
> have economic advantages. Resources--materials, time, per-
> sonnel, and equipment--constitute a limitation in any investiga-
> tion, and it is necessary to balance the information obtained
> against the expenditure. It may be that measuring only a
> sample instead of the entire population results in a margin
> of potential error, known as sampling error (referring to er-
> ror that in all probability might occur because of sampling
> not to error that necessarily has occurred or will occur be-
> cause of sampling), small enough for practical purposes--that
> is, small enough so that a reduction in this risk of error
> would not be worth the cost of achieving it by further observa-
> tions.

   Among the reasons for considering sampling is first that the
gain in accuracy from a complete count may not be worth the cost.
A second reason is that the individual measurements may not be as
accurate for a complete survey as for a sample. This is the case,
since a large number of measurements made hurriedly or super-
ficially may not represent as much true information as a small
number made carefully. A third reason is that a complete survey

may be impossible or extremely difficult because of the many items involved.

Before taking any measurements at all, however, it is desirable to make certain definitions, or have agreement on the beginning and end of a given collection or subject classification. We want to be sure that we measure, whether by sampling or complete enumeration, no more and no less than the collection with which we are concerned.

The individual collection can be suitably marked off by labelling the single or double-faced ranges with placards indicating the order or progression of the shelving. This may be a single sequence of numbers. This procedure will also be very helpful in the moving operation itself as a guide to the order in which the volumes should be withdrawn from the shelves, sections, and ranges. Further, the labelling procedure is especially important if we are dealing with a collection which is fragmented or shelved discontinuously or if the order of the materials is not easily discernible.

Instead of describing how the measurement is accomplished, it may be desirable to describe the preliminary steps for the measurement of the serial collection in the NLM as an example, and then summarize the procedure. The NLM serial collection was shelved, except for the separately shelved Japanese and Russian serial collections, in four large basic areas in the old NLM building. Three of these levels were in the form of tiers, one above the other, adjacent to the Main Reading Room; the fourth main area was some distance removed, in the basement. The four areas were approximately equal as can be determined from Table 1. The serial collection represented the major individual collection by far in terms of size; the 1961 NLM Annual Report indicated that there were 266,199 bound volumes plus additional material designated as 15,000 bound volume equivalents.

The procedure was, first of all, to determine the physical boundaries of this collection in terms of ranges and sections, ascertaining the beginning and ending points, and the shelving sequence. The one-fourth of the serial collection located in the base-

ment prompted some degree of caution in precisely determining the
physical boundary, inasmuch as the 19th century monograph collection was shelved close by, and the distinction between it and the
serial collection was not immediately apparent.

The next procedure was to take an inventory of the shelves in
the bookstack areas in which the serial materials were shelved.
This was conducted on a range-by-range (single-faced) basis starting at the beginning of the collection. All shelves in each single-
faced range were counted. Separate figures were kept, however,
for the non-empty shelves (those with some books on them) and the
empty shelves. All shelves minus empty shelves would yield the
number of non-empty shelves at the end of the inventory. The
number of non-empty shelves is a key figure in the measurement by
sampling process since this sets up the population of the group of
shelves with which we are concerned.

The inventory was accomplished by the use of a simple tally
sheet, each line of which served to designate a single-faced range.
On each line was indicated the total number of shelves and the
number of empty shelves, with another column for the number of
non-empty shelves. A sample tally sheet is illustrated as Figure
2.

Move Planning Form   Figure 2

Present building inventory of shelf capacity

Tally Sheet   Date:_____

Level:_____   Classification:_____

(1)	(2)	(3)	(4)
Designation of the Sin-gle-faced range	Total shelves	Empty shelves	Non-empty shelves
Sub-totals			

Note: Column No. 1 is simply for purposes of orientation in the inventory process; if the ranges are already numbered this is the designation to be used. If no numbering system exists a designation system of some kind should be employed to make sure of proper sequence in the inventory and the avoidance of duplication. The designation has the further advantage of facilitating rechecking of the figures.

To ascertain the total number of shelves (empty and non-empty) it is usually possible to ascertain the number of shelves per section (if constant) and the number of sections per single-faced range. The two figures can be multiplied to yield the total shelves in the single-faced range. If the number of shelves per section is not constant it is, of course, necessary to make a direct shelf-by-shelf count.

To ascertain the number of non-empty shelves, we can conveniently count the empty shelves--usually a very small figure-- and subtract from the count of total shelves. Thus, we have two passes involved here. However, both counts can be taken in one "pass" especially if there is lack of constancy with respect to number of shelves per section.

A combination of the two different ways was utilized in both the NLM and UCLA moves. A competent inventory taker, with good instruction and supervision, can get the feel of the counting operation and perform it quickly.

The figures obtained from the tally sheets (Figure 2) can be consolidated in terms of a given collection, or stack floor, on a form similar to "Inventory of shelf capacity in the present building, summary sheet" (Figure 3).

Normally we might express the total linear feet of non-empty shelves as: Number of non-empty shelves x 3 linear feet. This is not to say that this is the total of book material; rather it is the total linear feet of shelving. This is perfectly satisfactory if all of the shelves are of the same interior length. If they vary in length, as was the case in the NLM move operation, then it is necessary to categorize and identify the shelves with the corres-

Move Planning Form   Figure 3

Present building inventory of shelf capacity

Summary sheet

(1)	(2)	(3)	(4)	(5)	(6)
Classification (or collection)	Level(s) or floor(s)	Total Shelves	Empty Shelves	Non-empty shelves	Linear feet of non-empty shelves.*

*Column No. 5 multiplied by 3 linear feet, or, more precisely Column 5 X the shelf length in inches, divided by 12 inches.

ponding measurement, re-working our data slightly from Figure 3. Table 1 illustrates the management of data where shelves are of variable length; the form tabulates selected data from the NLM serial collection.

When shelves are of different length we can after tallying the total number of shelves for each dimension, secure a "weighted average shelf" for later use in the sampling routine. This may be expressed as follows:

$$150 \text{ shelves at } 36''$$
$$100 \text{ shelves at } 30''$$
$$50 \text{ shelves at } 24''$$

$$\frac{150 \times 36 + 100 \times 30 + 50 \times 24}{300} = \frac{9600}{300} = 32$$

Thus the interior length of 32 inches would express the average shelf length.

Table 1

Tabulation of selected data on National Library of Medicine
(NLM) serial collection

Classification (or collection)	Level	Shelf dimen- sion	Total shelves	Empty shelves	Non- empty shelves	Linear feet Non- empty shelves
Serials	Main	33.50	3,003	103	2,900	8,095.8
Serials	M-2	33.50	3,015	145	2,870	8,012.0
Serials	M-2	34.25	12	0	12	34.2
Serials	M-2	46.50	4	0	4	15.5
Serials	B-14	22.25	32	7	25	46.3
Serials	B-14	35.25	2,588	204	2,384	7,003.0

Preparation for sampling procedures

The total number of non-empty shelves gives us the population.
These shelves have varying numbers of books on them from, say,
one book measuring perhaps 1/4 inch in width up to a large number
of books aggregating perhaps 35 inches. We wish to secure a good
estimate of the extent of the book materials on all of the non-empty
shelves by sampling some of these shelves.

We want a random sample of the books on the (non-empty)
shelves. The significance of the word random is made clear in the
following statement: "Random as used in statistics is a technical
word; it has a meaning different from the one given in popular
usage. When a sample is called random, this describes not the
data in the sample, but the process by which the sample was obtained. Thus, randomness is a property not of an individual sample
but of the process of sampling, just as in a game of cards a fair
hand is not one in which the cards have certain values, but one
dealt by a certain process. In fact, what in card games is called

a fair hand is precisely what in statistical terminology would be called a random sample of the deck. A sample of size "n" is said to be a random sample if it was obtained by a process which gave each possible combination of "n" items in the population the same chance of being the sample actually drawn.

We will assume that the factor we are measuring, the number of linear inches of book material on shelf, is normally distributed in our population. Our sampling process can give us different degrees of reliability, that is, we can determine known probability limits by which our sample will vary from the true or actual total linear feet of book material on hand. We will discuss later what degree of accuracy we will want to have.

The measurement of the NLM serial collection may be used as an illustration at this point. The population of non-empty shelves was 11,175. The shelves were of varying interior length. It was decided to use a sample of 280 shelves. This sample size provided confidence limits such that 95 times out of 100 the variation from the true arithmetic mean (for the population) would not exceed 3 percent. A systematic sample was decided upon; this meant that every 40th shelf in this particular collection was examined and the linear inches of books recorded on a tally sheet. Shelf number 21 marked the beginning--21 was selected at random from a table of random numbers. Measurement consisted in pushing the volumes together, applying a book support, allowing for expansion, then measuring to the nearest half inch in decimal form on a tally sheet. The 280 samples yielded an aggregate of 7,880 inches of books. These data are summarized in Table 2.

Table 2

Data on sampling 280 shelves, NLM serial collection

Location	Number of shelves	Inches of book material
Main	74	2,224.50
M-1	73	2,051.50
M-2	72	1,831.00
B-14	61	1,781.00
Totals	280	7,880.00

We obtain $\frac{7,880''}{280}$ = 28.14", the arithmetic mean. We can then multiply the population of non-empty shelves (11,175) by the arithmetic mean (28.14") and divide by 12, which then yields 26,205 linear feet.

Alternatively, we can make use of the proportion between the linear inches of books in the sample shelves (7,880) and the linear inch capacity of the sample shelves (9,487) to secure an occupancy ratio, i.e., $\frac{7,880}{9,487}$ = 83.1. We know from the earlier measurement of shelves that the total non-empty shelves aggregated 31,526 linear feet. On the premise that the sample is representative of the population from which drawn, the 83.1 (percent) is applied against the linear feet of non-empty shelves, thus 83.1 x 31,526 linear feet = 26,198 linear feet book material.

As observed, we can compute the number of linear feet of books on the non-empty shelves in two ways. For example, let us assume we are given the population of 1,000 non-empty shelves for a given group of books (the shelves are 36" interior length), that a sample of 10 shelves was taken, that the sample yielded a total of 300 inches of book material.

1. Obtaining the estimated linear feet of book material by use of the sample arithmetic mean:-

$$\frac{300''}{10\text{ shelves}} = 30'' \text{ (the arithmetic mean)}$$

Population total of 1,000 shelves x 30" = 30,000"

$$\frac{30,000''}{12''} = 2,500 \text{ linear feet.}$$

2. Obtaining the estimated linear feet of book material by use of the sample proportion:-

$$\frac{300''}{10\text{ shelves x }36} = \frac{300}{360} = \frac{5}{6} \text{ (the proportion)}$$

1,000 shelves x 36" = 36,000

$$\frac{5}{6} \text{ x } 36,000 = 30,000$$

$$\frac{30,000}{12} = 2,500 \text{ linear feet.}$$

Requirements for accuracy in the measurement process

What sort of accuracy is required in the measurement of the
book collections? The answer to this question is conditioned by a
number of basic factors involved in the move planning and in the
method of moving itself. Thus, measurement, per se, must be
considered in the context of a number of facts and conditions. Study
of these facts lead us to the best possible answers regarding the
degree of accuracy needed.

An estimate of the total extent (linear feet) of the book collections to be moved is a central figure; the extent of space in the
new building is another key figure. These two figures govern what
we can and cannot do in the new building. The provision for growth
is dictated by these two figures; we may provide relatively larger
amounts of growth space for rapidly growing portions of the classification but always within the outer limits expressed by the capacity
of the new building. (Growth and its ramifications are discussed
later in the present Chapter and the distinction between actual capacity and practical capacity is described in Chapter IV.

An important factor in determining the relative accuracy needed is the methodology in moving books. This establishes a stacking
formula--the number of linear feet of books per section based on a
ratio between booktrucks and sections in the new building. This
ratio is changed in the course of the move, as necessary, to compensate for measurement error. The technique is described in
Chapter IV.

A good beginning in the measurement process is to calculate
the approximate size of the book collection to be moved, and the
amount of the shelf space in the new building. We know something
of the size of the book collection. This we derive from the total
number of shelves in the present building. We must bear in mind
books stored in locations other than in the main bookstacks. Later
a count of stored or "dummied out" material is added to the
totals derived from the sampling. The amount of material on hand
cannot exceed the number of shelves x 3 linear feet. Instead of 3
linear feet, a more precise statement would be the linear inch

length of the shelf. The amount of book material probably
does not vary appreciably from:

Number of shelves x 3 linear feet x .80 occupancy ratio. This
is to say that the building from which a move is being planned is
probably in crowded condition which means 80 percent occupancy.
The NLM and UCLA building occupancy ratios were between .80
and .85.

The amount of shelf space in the new building is derived from
the building plans. We can use either the total sections, which multiplied by the number of shelves per section and then by 3 yields
the total linear feet of shelf space. Thus, we have an outline, hazy
at this stage, but nonetheless a workable outline: the trial figure
of book material to be moved and the actual number of linear feet
of shelf space. (We will develop the notion of the section as the
usable unit of measurement for the new building instead of using
linear feet of shelf space.)

A factor which should be noted is that, in one sense, we will
be moving several book collections into the stack levels of the new
building. A certain group of LC subject classes or sub-classes will
go on the first stack level, another group on the second stack floor,
etc. We have, in other words, the problem of cutting off a subject
class or sub-class at the end of a stack floor. These are really
separate "targets". Before the move begins, we will, of course,
have decided upon the subject class arrangement by stack floor,
and in the move itself, we want to be sure to fit the designated
class or sub-class where indicated. This means we have several
problems in measurement. The decision regarding what classes will
be placed on the various floors is decided upon the basis of the
capacity of the stack floors in the new building, the desired growth
provision for the given subject class, and, of course, the size in
linear feet of the class, and the use of the collection.

A gross estimation can actually be made from the figures already on hand at this point:

Number of shelves x 3 linear feet x .80 occupancy
                                                    ratio,
(all arranged by sub-class).

Such a trial arrangement is, in fact, of value. Aside from setting
up a good working estimate of the collections, the procedure helps
define the relative accuracy we will need in our sample.

It should be mentioned that it is very desirable to end a given
stack floor with a sub-class (not splitting in the middle of the sub-
class). We will rarely find that there is a nice match between a
planned set of classes and sub-classes for a given floor; usually
there will be a bit of compressing or of loosening to achieve a
good ending on a stack floor. This is taken care of by varying the
stacking formula; it is achieved by the same method mentioned
above in compensating for error in measurement, namely, by varying the stacking formula so that we can end up exactly as planned
on each stack floor.

The factors mentioned are basic before we begin the subject of
sampling and the question of determining sample size. It is advisable at an early stage in the planning to secure the counsel of
a statistician regarding the sampling data assembled. We want to
think in terms of the subject class as a population, that is, the
non-empty shelves in Class A, Class B, etc., rather than in terms
of sub-class; in fact, we will attribute the sample arithmetic means
for the class as valid for the sub-classes of which they are part.
(Figures will be needed for sub-classes, of course, since frequently a stack floor will end with a sub-class rather than a class).

The reliability of a sample is shaped by the number of items
in the sample and by the variability of the spread of measurements
around the mean. In general, it can be said that a variation of $\pm$
3 percent is tolerable and is one for which we can compensate.

In the NLM and UCLA moves the data indicated that a sample
of 160 non-empty shelves would supply the $\pm$ 3 percent accuracy at
the .95 confidence level. The sampling should be tallied and the
arithmetic mean, standard deviation, standard error of the mean
computed with the advice of a statistician who will then be in a
position to advise on the need for additional sampling to reach $\pm$
3 percent or other desired accuracy. Done properly, the changes
are 95 out of 100 that our sample mean will not vary from the

true mean by more than plus or minus 3 percent.

Recording the results of the measurements

A systematic sample is most useful in developing the measurement of books on the non-empty shelves. Under this type of sampling every 10th or every 20th shelf, for example, would be examined and the linear inches of books recorded on a tally sheet.
The first shelf would be chosen at random and should be somewhere
near the beginning point of the subject class of the books and shelves
to be measured. For example, we assume that LC subject class P
comprises 5,250 non-empty shelves. We wish to take 200 samples.
Every "ith" shelf would be $\frac{5,250}{200}$ or 25. Every 25th shelf would be
inspected. The first shelf may be selected at random (from a table
of random numbers) but should be near the beginning of the shelving
in order that a full 200 samples are secured. Let us assume that
shelf number 10 is to be the beginning shelf, then every 25th shelf
thereafter would be examined until we have our full quota of 200
readings. The tally sheet for recording the samples is displayed
as Move Planning Form No. 4. (Figure 4).

The intensity of the compression exerted on the books occupying a given shelf will influence measurement. If a number of volumes are pressed together with great compression, then measured,
and then allowed to "expand", then measured a second time, we
might secure a measurement varying one inch (or more) from our
first measurement. How much compression should be applied before we make our measurement? One observation to be made is
that in the new building we will rarely pack books under extreme
compression, completely filling the shelves, in the new building
book shelves. The books on the new shelves will ordinarily be
"held together" by a bookend or book support. We might arbitrarily
describe this as a "normal" displacement of book shelf space. We
might, then, aim at measuring book materials in a manner which
will, as closely as possible, resemble the displacement on the
new shelves.

Figure 4

Sampling Tally Sheet for Measurement of the Book
Collections

Classification   Population: (Total number non-empty
(or collection):   shelves):

Interior length   Number of non-empty shelves in
of shelf (inches):   sample:

Staff member   Date sample taken:
taking sample:

Tally

Single-faced range designation consulted	shelf	Linear inches[1] book material on sample shelf
	1	
	2	
	3	
	4	
	5	
	6	
	7	
	8	
	9	
	0	
Sub-total		
Arithmetic mean		

[1]To be recorded decimally in intervals of half inches.

Our intent is to simulate normal array as closely as possible and also to create the same set of criteria for measurement of all the sample shelves.

The procedure, then, is: even up the books on the shelf, push the books firmly together, then insert a book support--allowing books to expand, then measure. Measurement is best made with a well-marked yardstick; the measurement should be expressed in units of one-half inch and recorded on a tally sheet of the sort illustrated in Figure 4 as a Move Planning Form. (The same book end or same type of book end should be used in all measurements).

This technique will have the effect of standardizing routines as closely as possible. There will, however, be some unavoidable distortion in measurement. In addition, some shelves in the sample may be completely filled and under extremely heavy compression-- somewhat more than if we were measuring their displacement under the "standard" conditions described above. It is suggested that in this case the shelf be recorded as equivalent to the shelf dimension itself, 35.0" or whatever its length. Another difficulty occurs when the shelf, although not completely filled, is nevertheless so occupied with books that a bookend cannot be placed in the space between the last book and the end of the shelf. In this event, it is suggested that the person taking the measurement simulate as closely as possible the pressure which would be exerted if the bookend could be used, then taking the measurement.

The total linear inches of books, recorded in all samples, is then divided by the number of samples. This gives us the arithmetic mean. The arithmetic mean multiplied by the population of non-empty shelves gives us the total linear inches of books, which, divided by 12 inches, gives us total linear feet of books. For example, let us assume Classification "K" comprises 301 non-empty shelves and that we have taken 50 samples. The total linear inches of the 50 sample shelves totals 1,675 linear inches. We divide 1,675 by 50 to obtain the arithmetic mean of 33.5 inches. We multiply the total of non-empty shelves, 301, by the arithmetic mean, 33.5 inches to obtain 10,083.5 inches, which, divided by 12 inches, yields 912 linear feet of books.

$$\frac{\text{Total linear inches of books in sample}}{\text{Number of sample shelves}} = \text{Arithmetic Mean (in inches)} \times \text{Total non-empty shelves} = \text{Total Linear Inches of Books}$$

$$\frac{\text{Total Linear Inches of books}}{12 \text{ Inches}} = \text{Total Linear Feet of Books}$$

The data should be secured for all subject classes and tabulated.

Other supplementary measurements

A library confronted with a move problem will probably have books in a variety of locations. While these may complicate the measurement operation they do not make it impossible.

Due to overcrowded conditions of the shelves, books may have been placed on the floor adjacent to the sections in which they would normally be shelved. Such books should be measured in complete form (not by sampling procedures) and the totals expressed in linear feet in terms of LC subject sub-class. The totals are then to be added to the estimates previously derived from the samples.

Other books may have been "dummied out," i.e., shelved in another location for lack of space at the precise classification point where shelving would normally occur, with a wooden block indicating the location of the long run or set. The measurement of such materials should cover all shelves, on a shelf-by-shelf basis (not by sampling procedures) and the totals expressed in linear feet in terms of LC subject sub-class. The totals are then to be added to the estimates previously derived from the samples. The integration of such "dummied out" books with the books from the main stacks, during the course of the move, is developed later in the text.

Thus, in summary we have:

(1) Books in the main stacks, estimates in linear feet obtained by sampling procedures;

(2)   Books "dummied out".   (3) Groups of books in other
                                  library buildings (for
                                  merging).

We will want to tabulate these data in a systematic readily
consulted form. The Boardmaster Control Board, or similar type
board, is of value here, inasmuch as the data can be displayed
easily and the individual figures can be removed and replaced by
later figures.

Move Planning Form   Figure 5

Summary of measurements of the book collections
(linear feet)

Sub-class	Main bookstacks	Dummied out (various locations)	Library No. 1 (to be merged)	Total

Books which are in circulation (and on interlibrary loan) represent a somewhat different problem. Is the number of books in circulation at approximately the same level throughout the year? If the
number of books in circulation is at a fairly constant level throughout the year, we could safely measure what is on shelf, that is,
not consider the books in circulation as a measurement factor at
all. This hypothesis bears checking in the individual library environment.

Following the end of the semester at a college or university,
it is very likely that the inventory is relatively larger, especially
for certain of the Library of Congress subject classes. However,

the variability in bookstock during the year may not be sufficiently
high to disturb our estimates of the size of the collection in linear
feet; our basic purpose is the measurement of the total linear
footage of a collection.

Summary of measurement procedure

(1) The total number of non-empty shelves should be
determined. This total should take into account the non-standard
shelves. Data is presented in terms of classes and sub-classes
(or collection designation) showing location.

(2) Determine number of samples to be taken. Samples
may be taken in terms of LC classification (or for entire collection).

(3) Calculate estimates in linear feet for the various
classifications.

(4) Measure residual materials "dummied out" volumes,
books in other library buildings for merging with main group,
etc., adding results to figures for main collection.

The growth of book collections

Study of the growth of the individual LC classifications or sub-
classes (or other collections or entities of books) is important in
order to make adequate shelving provision in the new building.
Since collections or classifications may well vary in their rate of
growth, the investigation should be in terms of classes, sub-
classes, or the individual entity of books concerned.

Unless we have an adequate idea of the growth characteristics
we can make only imperfect provision for arrangement of the collections in the new building. As mentioned, the annual reports may
be a source of data; the greater the detail of reporting in terms of
individual collections the better we are able to establish the growth
rates. We have already mentioned the possible limitation of the annual report figures giving the size of the collections by having
stated that the measurement of the collections cannot usefully be
transacted in terms of volumes reported. This difficulty inherent in
the concept volume is also evident when we consider growth; how-

ever, we can make limited use of the different yearly totals established in volumes or pieces. If we have data for a number of
years, expressed in volumes or pieces we can draw some conclusions with respect to growth. It is desirable to state what the
figures do not tell us, however. If we take figures say of the last
10 years, we are essentially describing what the growth in terms
of volumes or pieces has been over that period of time. Will this
same pattern persist in the future? The answer to this will vary
with the individual library; if acquisitions funds are relatively
stable (aside from nominal increases in dollar amount to provide
stable purchasing power) then we might well use our data more
comfortably in portraying future trends; if however, the book funds
will be substantially larger and if there is a firm intent to speed
up the addition to the collections we must use our growth figures
as minimal ones and with considerably greater caution.

Significance and ramification of growth

The library concerned with a move problem must examine the characteristics of its various classifications or collections to assure adequate provision for such growth in its new building. We may speak of growth in two distinct ways. First, we may
speak of the net increase in number of volumes or the net increase
in number of linear feet annually; secondly, we may consider growth
in the context of a rate of change annually and speak of growth on
the order of an annual percentage.

We may examine these two ways by recourse to actual data.
The NLM collection of serials was counted in terms of the number
of volumes in 1954. This was the basic count and the annual increments were added to this base, as portrayed in Table 3.

The growth in terms of amount of change varies from a net
addition of 5,858 volumes in 1955 to a high of 9,552 volumes in
1957. The arithmetic mean or average of the additions to the serial
collection (the additions 1955 through 1960 divided by 6 years) is
7981 volumes.

The growth in terms of a rate, based on the 1954 beginning
point, can be computed by use of the compound interest formula.

This will provide average annual percent of change. This type of
growth is handled by the formula $P_n = P_0 (1 + r)^n$, where P_n is
equivalent to the number of volumes at the end of the period being
treated, P_0 is equivalent to the number of volumes at the beginning
of the period, "r" equals the rate of change, and "n" equals the
number of years. Thus.

$$259,066 + 211,178 (1 + r)^6$$
$$\log 259,066 + \log 211,178 + 6 \log (1 + r)$$

$$r = 3.5 \text{ percent}$$

Table 3

Growth of the NLM serial collection

Year	Volumes added	Volumes withdrawn	Net Volumes added	Total volumes	Actual increase over previous yr.
1954	---	---	---	211,178	
1955	5,858	0	5,858	217,036	2.8
1956	6,955	0	6,955	223,991	3.2
1957	9,552	0	9,552	233,543	4.3
1958	8,406	0	8,406	241,949	3.4
1959	9,299	478	8,821	250,770	3.6
1960	8,495	199	8,296	259,066	3.3

The average annual rate of change works out to be 3.5 percent
with reference to the base year, 1954. The notion of constant ratio
of change over a period of years signifies an increasing amount of
change each year. In the present figures we can see that, in precise terms, this is not the case. We have a spotty picture characterized by an increasing amount for one year, followed by a de-
creasing or lower amount the next year.

Library statistics should be examined to determine what the
growth has been. What it will be may be quite different. The aver-

age annual growth which describes the past years activity may de-
cline; the individual library characteristics, in the final analysis
must be taken in conjunction with the lesson to be learned from
the past year's figures. Plans for microfilming, shifts in collection policy, budgetary changes -- all these will place a most important part in the reckoning of growth. The data for past years
merely help us place the problem in perspective.

A further interesting illustration of book collection growth is
provided by examination of the University of California (Los Angeles)
Library statistics recounting the total volumes on hand since fiscal
year 1955. These figures are set for in Table 4.

Table 4

Growth of UCLA Library book collections
since 1955
(average annual growth of 6.38 percent)

Year	Volumes added	Percent increase (Actual)	Actual total volumes	Hypothetical total volumes at 6.38 percent annually
1955			1,114,876	
1956	64,998	5.8	1,159,723	1,186,005
1957	68,612	5.9	1,213,238	1,261,672
1958	75,265	6.1	1,301,075	1,342,166
1959	81,641	6.3	1,379,168	1,427,796
1960	90,845	6.6	1,464,474	1,518,889
1961	105,995	7.2	1,568,565	1,615,794
1962	154,801	9.9	1,719,359	1,718,882

Here the base year was chosen as 1955 because the acquisitions funds for the period 1955 - 1962 were in fairly good correspondence; prior to 1955 the funds were lower and the magnitude of
acquisitions was not typical of the trend for 1955 and later. Since
1955 there has been an increasing number of volumes added (the

actual rate rises slightly as well). An average annual rate of 6.38 percent is descriptive of this curve; we can observe how nicely the 6.38 percent fits by simply using the holdings of 1955 and applying the 6.38 percent (as in compound interest) each year.

The rate of increase which will obtain is not entirely of course a statistical matter but is rather related to the input of resources to increase the collections, the number of gifts, the collection policy, and manpower resources to process the intake into the collections, and by other special considerations. It should be emphasized, too, that exponential growth curves "level off", i.e., the rate of increase tends to slow down. Thus, the tables illustrating varied rates of growth (cf. Table 6) must be read in the light of the individual library's program. The plans for expansion will affect the growth curve.

As previously mentioned it may be desirable to have data in terms of individual collections (classes or sub-classes) rather than on the basis of the Library's entire collections. If individual additions to the various classifications are available, they should be studies for the recent past. The UCLA figures indicated volumes added according to LC subject class. They provided a good basis for inspecting the nature of growth in terms of the individual subject classes. Growth figures are presented in Table 5.

The foregoing summary on growth of the library's book collection was provided as an aid in securing the best indication of the rate for the various portions of the collection. Such a finding is of course necessary in order that adequate provision for growth be made in the new building bookstacks.

Thus, available statistical material will have to be studied carefully. In general, the larger the number of consecutive years for which volume counts are available the better. The questions to be asked, within the context of such figures, are: What trends are exhibited? Does the increase appear to be in terms of a constant rate of change (i.e. an increasing amount of change annually? An estimate of future behavior of a trend will have to be considered as well when we make final provision for growth.

Table 5

Growth of Classes A and H since 1955, UCLA Library

CLASS A

Fiscal Year	Volumes added	Total volumes	Present increase
1955	---	39,321	---
1956	1,683	41,004	4.28
1957	1,950	42,954	4.75
1958	1,332	44,286	3.10
1959	1,879	46,165	4.42
1960	2,132	48,297	4.61
1961	2,956	51,253	4.82
1962	4,199	55,452	5.12

CLASS H

Fiscal Year	Volumes added	Total volumes	Present increase
1955	---	83,362	---
1956	6,237	89,599	7.48
1957	6,224	95,823	6.94
1958	7,520	103,343	7.84
1959	8,417	111,760	8.14
1960	9,106	120,866	8.14
1961	9,585	130,451	7.93
1962	12,169	142,620	9.32

The UCLA statistics reflect a growth at more nearly a constant rate (6.83 percent average annual growth), although the actual increase each year is higher. There should be a word of caution on the constant rate or exponential curve: it signifies a heavier and heavier intake of volumes, which must eventually level off.

The implications of a constant rate of growth are spelled out in Table 6 which sets out the results of growth at various rates

Table 6

Tabulation of Various Growth Rates Over 10 Year Period

Year	1.0 percent		2.0 percent		3.0 percent		4.0 percent		5.0 percent	
	Net lin. ft. added	Total lin. ft.	Net lin. ft. added	Total lin. ft.	Net lin. ft. added	Total lin. ft.	Net lin. ft. added	Total lin. ft.	Net lin. ft. added	Total lin. ft.
0	0	10,000	0	10,000	0	10,000	0	10,000	0	10,000
1	100	10,100	200	10,200	300	10,300	400	10,400	500	10,500
2	101	10,201	204	10,404	309	10,609	416	10,816	525	11,025
3	102	10,303	208	10,612	318	10,927	433	11,249	551	11,576
4	103	10,406	212	10,824	328	11,255	450	11,699	579	12,155
5	104	10,510	216	11,040	337	11,592	468	12,167	605	12,763
6	105	10,615	221	11,261	348	11,940	487	12,654	638	13,401
7	106	10,721	225	11,486	358	12,298	506	13,160	670	14,071
8	107	10,828	230	11,716	369	12,667	526	13,686	704	14,775
9	108	10,936	234	11,950	380	13,047	547	14,233	739	15,514
10	109	11,045	239	12,189	391	13,438	569	14,802	776	16,290

over a 10 year period. This Table illustrates the growth in linear
feet;   the interpretation, of course, holds for volumes as well.
One further point should be made: if we consider a relatively small
collection and the base year is fairly recent then our resultant
average annual percent of growth may be quite large. On the other
hand if we have a relatively large collection and the base year is
fairly remote then the average annual percent of growth may be
relatively small. Thus, the percent of growth per se is not important; it becomes important when the base year and the size of the
collection are considered.

Making the future growth projection

We can estimate future growth by using the measurement of
the collections (calculated in terms of linear feet by means of
sample procedures and measurement procedures described) in conjunction with the percentage of growth (calculated from inspection
of past years' reporting of volumes or pieces on hand). This is an
approximation. We do not have data on recent years' growth in
terms of linear feet, but only in terms of volumes or pieces. We
are approximating by stating that the rate of past growth found to
exist in recent years with respect to volumes will be characteristic
of the future growth in terms of linear feet.
(This assumes that in the past there existed a good correlation between the rate of growth, in terms of volumes, and the rate of
growth, in terms of linear feet, which may not be exactly correct.
We can't be certain that if the average growth in terms of volumes
was 2 percent that the average growth was 2 percent also in terms
of linear feet.)

The projection of growth, however, cannot be based on this
statistical aspect alone. A number of other events have to be considered. The growth of a given library's collections is a reflection
of a number of ingredients: the dollar input into the acquisitions
program, the collection policy (and its relative stability over the
years), the manpower input and efficiency in the technical processes

Figure 6

GRAPH PROJECTING AT ANNUAL RATE OF 4 PERCENT

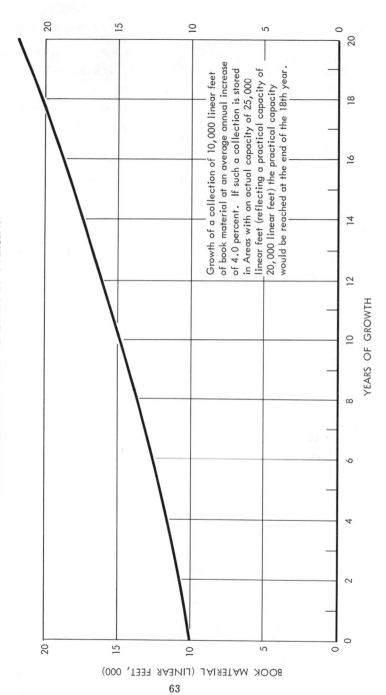

Growth of a collection of 10,000 linear feet of book material at an average annual increase of 4.0 percent. If such a collection is stored in Areas with an actual capacity of 25,000 linear feet (reflecting a practical capacity of 20,000 linear feet) the practical capacity would be reached at the end of the 18th year.

YEARS OF GROWTH

BOOK MATERIAL (LINEAR FEET, 000)

and other factors. The fortuitous aspect of extensive gifts, either
in dollars or in book materials, introduces an additional element.

These factors are mentioned because they were contributory
to the annual increments of volumes added and to a resultant rate
of growth. The question to be asked is, to what extent will these
factors influence the rate of growth which we found to be characteristic of the past? Will there be changes in the dollar input for
the acquisitions program, changes in collection policy, etc. ? Is the
size of the collection, by decision, to level off at a certain point
in time? This sort of examination may be subjective and circum-
stantial, but the process of review to formalize and define the
probable future shape of the library's collections can be of considerable help in making a good decision regarding the best possible deployment of the book collections in the new building bookstack areas.

The characteristics of a given collection of book materials
can be conveniently worked out in the Move Planning Form (Figure
7). Once we have measured a given collection in linear feet and
have a growth rate, we can plot the growth and get an idea of its
size in 5, 10 or other number of years desired.

The degree of use sustained by different collections

As one of the findings in developing a history of the characteristics of the various collections, we can take up the question of the
degree of use, that is, the relative difference in circulation or loan
demand for one particular class of materials over another. The
survey of use can proceed at various levels of intensity or refinement, depending upon the time available. The survey of use is of
value and importance when we discuss the optimum placement of
the collections in the new bookstack areas--more significantly when
we consider a closed stack library. (An open stack library may be
committed to classification ordering of the books on the shelves.)
The use pattern may, in part, be determined from examination of
the circulation statistics; these statistics may be studied from the
standpoint of the number of uses each of these collections has experienced during a stated time period. Such an examination may re-

Move Planning Form   Figure 7

Size of collections and the growth rate

Classification on classification:

Present size in linear feet:

Annual growth rate:

Estimate of size of collection or classification at time of move.

If the time of measurement is sometime before the move, then the
growth rate should be used to compute the estimated size of the
collection at the time of the move. For example, assume a collection measuring 5,000 linear feet, an annual growth rate of 4 percent, and the time between measurement and move as 6 months.

Then: $5,000 \times \frac{.04}{2} = 100$ linear ft. of growth, to be added to the
5,000 linear feet, yielding new total of 5,100 linear feet.

Extrapolation of collection or classification at annual growth rate:

Year	Starting size (linear feet)	Additions (linear feet)	Ending size (linear feet)
1			
2			
3			
4			
5			

late to portions of an individual collection (e.g., based on time
period of the published materials, or a specific portion of the
classification). Another use to be made of such findings is the
question of splitting or segmenting a collection, dependent upon the
degree of use. (The NLM survey of the serial collection, based on
interlibrary loan use, provided the basis for segmenting the serial
collection on the basis of time period.)

Over-size books

Terminology will differ as to what constitutes an over-size
volume. We use here the ALA definition as set forth in Glossary

<u>of</u> <u>Library</u> <u>Terms.</u> Variable, too, will be individual library prac-
tices as to storing such volumes. In the old building, the NLM collection of 20th century monographs, for example was segmented by
size, into the octavo collection and the quarto collection. The call
number was suffixed with an "o" or a "q".

Table 7

Characterization of book sizes at National Library of Medicine
and UCLA Library

UCLA Library	NLM
25 cm. and under	25 cm. and under
Not designated	Not designated
25.5 cm. to 38 cm.	More than 25 cm. but less than 36 cm.
Designated by single asterisk adjacent to call number	Regarded as quarto and letter "q" placed in front of Cutter number
38.1 cm. to 61 cm. Designated by double asterisk adjacent to call number	More than 36 cm. Regard as folio and the letter "f" placed in front of Cutter number
More than 61 cm. Designated by triple asterisk next to call number	

The reason for the decision to change this was the fact that
the quartos could be shelved with octavos in the new building because the spacing of shelves in the new building (approximately 13
inches clear space) would accommodate either. Another important
factor was the superior circulation control which could be exerted over
a unified collection. (Errors in shelving quartos in the octavo area,
and octavos in the quarto area had not been uncommon in the old
building.)

It may be found that many small volumes are shelved in the
large volume area. This was true in both the NLM and UCLA and
stems from the practice of shelving all volumes of a set together
even though they vary in size. Therefore, if a part of a set is

quarto, all in the set are marked for quarto shelving. As a part
of the move planning the facts should be checked to ascertain the
desirability for continuing the separation by size of the book, assuming there is such segregation in effect.

A test to be considered in possible merger of octavos and
quartos in the new building is the height of the books. As a general rule, the integration of "large" and "small" volumes can proceed if the 12 inches of clear space between shelves is an appropriate free space on a 90" high shelving with base and 6 adjustable
shelves). The adjustment of a small number of shelves, on an ad
hoc basis is practicable. During the NLM and UCLA moves, adjustments were made without difficulty. It will be perhaps found
that a number of volumes will be large volumes not classed as
over size. This was the case in the NLM and UCLA moves: where
there was a marked concentration of tall volumes (in excess of 12
inches in height) the sections were changed from 6 adjustable
shelves to 5 adjustable shelves. This occurred in the UCLA move,
especially for the beginning of Class J and in Class N, and in the
NLM move with respect to the collection of documents.

Miscellaneous collections of books

There will, in all probability, be a number of collections of
books in various offices (Librarian, Department Heads, etc.) as
well as small working collections (reference collections in the
Acquisitions Department, collections shelved adjacent to the desks
of catalogers, etc.).

Measurement in such cases can proceed quite simply, and unless large expansion is a factor, the counting may be taken approximately in terms of the number of shelves of book materials which
exist in the different collections. The important factor, however,
is that adequate space exist in the new building for such materials,
that is, that the newly assigned offices have sufficient space to
house the collections to be moved, with sufficient space for desired
expansion. However, it will be desirable to place in the main collections those volumes which are no longer required in special collections well in advance of move time.

This has the desirable effect of placing the volumes in the main stacks for measurement of the basic collections already discussed. Any large augmentation of the main stack collection should, of course, be made prior to the measurement of the main book collections.

Alternatively, these volumes could be placed in the exchange duplicates. In either case this operation can be accomplished in conjunction with the house cleaning operation already described.

The exchange duplicates

If the exchange duplicates can remain in the present buildings the problem of moving is non-existent. If, however, the duplicates will have to be moved to the new building, it is then desirable to study the ways and possible means to reduce such materials to a minimum to avoid transportation to the new building. It will ordinarily be less costly to send out exchange materials than to move them to the new building (and then dispatch them to exchange partners).

Similarly, the requests for incoming material on exchange must be studied and arrangements made to delay such deliveries after a certain point in time, and then have the material delivered to the new building. Thus, a library planning a move might stop (insofar as possible) exchange deliveries to it, say, three months prior to the move, having made arrangements for delivery to the new building.

Special forms of library material

Special forms of library material include maps, charts, motion pictures, microfilms, fine prints, phonodiscs, and phototapes. The measurement of such materials is best carried out by complete inventory of material on hand and by study of its special characteristics in conjunction with the ordering of shelving or containers to house it in the new building.

The provision of space for such materials will vary within the individual library. Of importance, also, are the plans of the individual library with respect to augmenting such collections during future years. In taking cognizance of growth, there must be a

reckoning of the special equipment necessary for housing such items
as maps, charts, etc., commensurate with the collecting policy
that will be followed over the coming years. Hence, no precise
or developed procedure for measurement can be introduced here.
The basic essentials, however, can be re-asserted: the amount of
material on hand, so many folios, maps, motion pictures, etc.
has to be established. The relationship of the material on hand to
the present housing (shelving) capability has to be studied. How
much additional housing, if any, is required to take care of what
is on hand at the present time? In addition, what are the future
plans with respect to the collection of special forms of material?
This will play a part in the provision for housing space in the new
building. Finally, how much special shelving is required to take
care of what we have on hand and how much should have, in addition, to absorb growth? Probably a good deal of the special equipment, such as filing cases for maps, will be moved to the new
building. The relative crowding of such cabinets and the future collecting plans, will dictate how many additional cases should be on
hand. The orders for the desired equipment should be checked, of
course, to ensure their delivery well in advance of moving time.

Rare books

The moving of rare books calls for special safeguards. Care
in physical handling, accuracy in the control of the records, and
adequate security provisions to avoid loss or damage, are essential. From the standpoint of controls and safeguards the move of
the National Library of Medicine collection of rare books may be
of interest. This collection, comprising 35,000 volumes, is under
the jurisdiction of the History of Medicine Division; it was located
in Cleveland, Ohio, and was moved to the new building in Bethesda
at the time the move of the main collection was being executed.

It was decided in planning for the move of the History of Medicine division that the presence of each book be established. This
was done for the Incunabula Collection, the Sixteenth and Seventeenth
Century books and, partly, for the Eighteenth Century Collection.
The basis for this check was the shelf list. One of the several

reasons for establishing the presence of the books is, of course, to make certain before the move what is in the library.

Procedurally, the shelflist was microfilmed and two Xerox copies of each of the cards was produced. One set of cards was used to compile the inventory; the other set was used for the books, one copy of each card being inserted in the book to which it related. Each set of cards was first given the same serial order numbers.

Measurement of the book collections was handled on a shelf by shelf basis in terms of linear inches; normally rare book collections are so small that sampling procedures would not be required. Furthermore, the measurement can be accomplished in conjunction with other operations in preparing rare books for moving, for example, the inventory process just mentioned. The use of book-trucks in the manner described in this text would not be appropriate. Undue compression of the books would probably not be advisable. Other means are available, including properly constructed cardboard containers.

Consideration should be given the individual wrapping of books. In the NLM move of the History of Medicine Division materials the incunabula, 16th, 17th century books were wrapped in heavy kraft paper. The 18th century books were wrapped selectively (material in poor condition, etc.).

In the NLM move, waterproof cardboard containers (approximately 20" x 18" x 12") were used. The books were packed into the containers in serial number order by the mover, under the supervision of a library staff member. When the box was filled, it was sealed in the presence of the Library staff member, who recorded that books covered by, say, serial numbers 1-42 were in Box no. 1, etc. Since the boxes as well as the moving vans were sealed and seals on the moving vans were broken at the new building in the presence of library staff, the check-off in the new building could be accomplished in terms of the numbered boxes rather than in terms of individual books. In library moves of rare book materials there should be a system of control which certifies that books have been packed at the sending point; the same system should provide for checking off the materials at the receiving point.

The receipt of the boxes thus constituted the end of the move. The books were not unwrapped by the mover (in fact, this was not part of the contract). The unwrapping should be conducted under the most secure conditions possible, by responsible staff members. Wrappings and boxes should not be discarded until double-checked by a responsible member of the rare books department staff.

Consideration should also be given to the insurance of the books and security controls to guard against loss and theft should be carefully planned and periodically checked.

Changes in the arrangement of the book collections

The move should be regarded as a means by which a superior arrangement of the book collections can be effected. This arrangement may involve, for example, the bringing together of separately maintained collections of octavos and quartos. It may involve, on the other hand, a separation of an existing collection.

It may be designed to concentrate the more heavily used portion of a collection into a smaller shelving area near the point of service. This was the rationale for splitting the NLM serial collection.

The placement of books in strategic locations (whether this is combined or not with a merger of collections is an element to consider. The factor here is degree of use and proximity to service point (or book lift, or service elevator). The kinds of arrangements and ways in which to bring them about are discussed in the following pages.

The merger of different collections or groups of books

Merger simply signifies the bringing together or consolidation of book collections shelved separately in the present building for one or more reasons. The merger can occur before, during, or after the main move. The purpose of a merger is to correct undesirable separations of book collections or of miscellaneous groups of books. Such mergers may vary in magnitude, from the consolidation of two relatively large collections to the integration of small

quantities of books which have had to be "dummied out" to separate
locations for want of shelf space. Mergers can be considered also
in terms of bringing isolated materials back into their normal
shelving place, or can involve basic policy issues where the possible merger of two large collections are involved, e.g., in the
National Library of Medicine move, the policy decision was made
to merge the 20th Century Monograph Collection which in the old
building was separately shelved, the octavos in one location, the
quartos in another.

The vital consideration involved is that the move should be
looked upon as a means by which a superior arrangement of the
collections can be achieved. Generally, the separation of book
collections or groups of miscellaneous books had their origin in
the lack of space for a more desirable arrangement. More often
than not the move to the new building will provide the opportunity
to make suitable corrections.

The merger of book materials may be handled in a number of
ways. The choice among the alternatives is dictated by the extent
of the book materials, their location, distance, time, space
availability and other factors. As a convenience in terminology,
we can speak arbitrarily of a "major" group representing the
numerically larger group of books, and a "minor" group, the
numerically smaller group of books, and we can, further, speak
of merging the minor group with the major group. The different
ways to handle the merger are: (1) the minor group is shelved with
the major group in advance of the move; (2) blending the minor
group into the major group during the move by bringing the minor
group, in logical instalments, to the place in the present building
bookstacks where the major group is in the process of being loaded onto booktrucks; (3) the merger can be accomplished by placing
markers at points in the major group (in the present building bookstacks), the markers indicating the number of sections to be left
vacant in the new building bookstacks. The number of sections reserved is determined, of course, by the extent (linear feet) of the
parts of the minor group to be moved; the minor group is moved

after the main move and is fitted into the sections reserved with a
minimum of shifting; (4) sections can be left vacant in the new
building on a periodic basis, every "i" th section, such that the
major group moves first, followed by the minor group which then
fits in, with moderate shifting, into the sections left vacant on a
periodic basis; (5) merger can be handled after the move by having
the major group move first to the new building, then the minor
group moved. Volumes constituting the minor group are then simply
reshelved on a volume-by-volume basis. These methods can now
be set forth in detail and their advantages and disadvantages established.

(Method 1) Merger in advance of the move

Generally, if space, work force, and time permit, the merging should be accomplished before the move even if the merging
has the effect of severely loading (or over-loading) the sections
receiving the merged materials.

An extensive merger was accomplished at the National Library
of Medicine prior to move. The 20th Century Monograph Collection
was shelved in two separate (but adjacent) locations, the octavos in
one area, the quartos in another . This separation had been initiated in past years to conserve space. It was decided that the two
separate collections should be consolidated in the new building and
that the merger should be accomplished prior to the move.

On the basis of the measurement techniques already described,
the figures set forth in Table 8 were developed.

The development of these and other data will perhaps be of
interest in parallel situations. For the octavos, the occupancy
ratio (the total linear feet of material divided by the total linear
feet of shelving) was 75.8 percent, a crowded condition, but nonetheless one in which some maneuverability was present. With respect to the quartos, the occupancy ratio, on the other hand, was
a very heavy 90.6 percent. The arithmetic indicates that the total
shelves in the octavo area 3,316 multiplied by 3 linear feet pro-
duces a total of 9,948 linear feet of shelf space. The measurement
of the octavos (6,619 feet) plus the quartos (1,632 linear feet) totals

Table 8

Tabulation of data on the National Library of Medicine
20th Century monograph collection

	Octavos	Quartos	Totals
Total number of shelves	3,316	615	--
Total number of non-empty shelves	2,970	613	--
Total number of empty shelves	346	2	--
Linear feet of books	6,619	1,632	8,251
Occupancy ratio	75.8	90.6	82.9

Note: The shelves were 36 inch interior dimension; the occupancy
ratio therefore was for the octavos:

$$\frac{6,619 \text{ linear feet of books}}{3 \text{ linear feet x } 3,316 \text{ total shelves}} = 75.8$$

only 8,251 linear feet, which indicates sufficient space. Yet this
fact alone would not have provided sufficient basis for an affirma-
tive decision on merger. The question was the distribution of the
free space in the octavo shelving, and the distribution pattern of
books in the subject classification for both the octavos and the
quartos. In other words, it was not sufficient for free space per
se to exist in the octavo area but that it be evenly distributed;
secondly, the number of books per given subject classification for
both octavos and quartos would have to be in approximately the
same pattern. There should not be, for example, a very heavy
concentration of quartos in one subject classification area, for this
would mean extensive shifting of octavos. Fortunately, the free
space was distributed, if not in an ideal pattern, at least not concentrated in large groups in the octavo shelving area; in addition,
by inspection of the shelf list and inspection of the books on the

shelves it was deduced that the relationship of books to any particular subject point in the classification was fairly good.

Method 2: Blending the minor group into the major group during the move

In the UCLA Library (old building) a large group of books were
"dummied out" to remote locations, in some instances the same
stack level, but in other cases different stack levels. Of a grand
total of 68,000 linear feet of regular size books there were a total
of 3,416 linear feet (roughly 35,000 volumes) dummied out in the
minor group. The extent of this is shown in Table 9.

Table 9

Distribution of "dummied out" books by subject class, UCLA
Library

Subject Class	Linear feet
A	1021
B	711
C	24
D	432
E	4
F	2
G	30
H	182
J	326
K	10
P	307
U	22
Z	267
Total	3416

Most of the 3,416 linear feet was made up of sets, in fact, a
total of 2,600 linear feet comprised sets of 2 linear feet and larger.
The technique is to "blend in" the dummied out materials, constituting the minor group, at the precise time the move operation had
reached the classification point in the major group represented by

the given set which was "dummied out".

Characteristics which would make Method 2 practicable for a minor group is the presence of large groups of books relating to a specific point--a single call number--in the classification. The fact that there existed some 3,400 linear feet of book materials dummied out would not, per se, make blending an economical operation.

Sets aggregating 2 linear feet or more would be good candidates for blending. The second characteristic is that of transportation: the minor group ought to be capable of being readily brought to the point of operations of the major group.

Increments of less than 2 linear feet each, within the minor group, can be handled by Method 5, basically a shelving operation.

In the planning for Method 2, it is essential to take an inventory of the "dummed out" material. Such an inventory is conveniently accomplished by using cards (Figure 9) which contain space to record the call number and the extent in linear inches (or feet) of each item.

Figure 8

Move Planning Form

Card (3"x5") for recording data regarding dummied
out books

SUB-CLASS	TOTAL LINEAR INCHES	TOTAL LINEAR FEET	LOCATION OF MATERIAL	DUMMY IN PLACE (CHECK)
AP2 L87		8	L-5	
COMMENT				

The data from the cards can be made into a list of sets which each aggregate 2 linear feet or more (or whatever breaking point desired). Alternatively, the cards themselves could constitute such a list or inventory (Figure 10). The inventory of blends is impor-

tant for the Library stack supervisor to have to alert him to the
imminence of a "blend."

Figure 9

Move Planning Form

Inventory of Blends

Call Number	Extent (linear feet)	Location
AP 20. R314	12	Level 3 (cage)
AP 22. R324	23	Level 3 (cage)

Method 3: Merging by designating specific Sections vacant during the move operation

The books constituting the minor group may be in a separate
building making blending quite difficult. The method here described
designates as vacant certain sections (in the new building) commensurate with the number of linear feet involving a specific call
number. The characteristics that make this method profitable are
the fact that the material is in the form of sets (here in increments larger than, say, 5 linear feet), and the books are either
located in another (distant) building or it is otherwise impracticable
to use Method 2 (blending).

Procedurally, this method is worked out by having a placard
about 10" x 14" inserted in the major group at the classification
point concerned. The placard, which should be easily visible to the
stack supervisor, indicates (a) the call number; (b) the extent of
the set in linear feet; (c) the number of sections it is decided to
leave vacant in the new building. This placard remains on the booktruck and it constitutes a directive to the stack supervisor in the
new building that the indicated number of sections be left vacant as
soon as the booktruck containing the placard has been emptied into
its appropriate section.

Recording of the data on the sets to be handled under this method is in the form of cards (Figure 10) amended to indicate name

of the building where books are located and then in list form. The
list is for the stack supervisors in the old and the new building.

Figure 10

Move Planning Form

Inventory of Sections to be left Empty in new building
Books now located_____

Call number	Extent (linear feet)	Sections to be left empty

This method can be seen graphically by turning to a specific
move operation, the Institute of Industrial Relations Library at
UCLA. This library was located in a building separate from the
new building. It was to be integrated into the main collections.
Its holdings were heavily concentrated in the LC H Classification,
as indicated by Table 10.

It is to be noted in Table 10 that HD consisting of 899 linear
feet constituted 57 percent of the total linear feet of book material
in the IRR Library, that all of Class H represented 83 percent of
the total.

Further, when sets comprising five linear feet and more were
tabulated, the data shown in Table 11 was obtained.

Thus, Method 3 (the designation of specific Sections to remain
vacant) was desirable. For the materials which aggregated under
5 linear feet Method 4 (the designation of Sections to remain vacant
on a periodic basis) was used for the HD class. With respect to
other than class HD, Method 5 was used.

Another instance where the use of Method 3 is applicable oc-

Table 10

Measurement of books in Library of the Institute of
Industrial Relations, UCLA

Subject Class	Linear feet book material
A	14
B	16
C	4
D	11
E	17
F	25
G	2
H	16
HA	14
HB	84
HC	109
HD	899
HE	10
HF	72
HG	29
HM	16
HN	8
HQ	7
HS	3
HT	4
HV	14
HX	19
J	37
K	18
L	15
M	1
P	8
Q	4
S	4
T	40
U	3
V	31
Z	13
Total	1567

Table 11

Inventory of sets and decision on number of empty sections
Institute of Industrial Relations Library, UCLA
(Sets 5 lin. ft. and over)

Classification	Linear feet
HA 1 A51	5
HB 1 A511	6
HB 1 H511	10
HD 4935 U543	7
HD 5503 A34a	22
HD 5503 A7223	28
HD 5503 A724a-1	12
HD 6350 (all)	100
HD 6350 P9T9	17
HD 6515 (all)	72
HD 7801 I615	6
HD 8051 M76	11
HD 8051 U585b	35
HD 8055 A51RP	6
HD 8101 A3	18
HF 5001 B97	20
HF 5001 F77	15
HG 1 C73	24
K1 Y12	5 Total 419

curs when it is by design that we wish to merge the minor group
with the major at a later date. A "core" group of journals was
maintained in the UCLA Library "old" building adjacent to the Circulation Desk.

It was desired to maintain these journals in place until close to
the time at which the new building would be the center of library
operations. However, these journals, mainly in the AP 2 and AP 4
Library Congress classification, aggregating some 375 linear feet
were to be shelved in the main stacks in the new building. Thus,
Method 3 was utilized conveniently.

Method 4: Merging by designating Sections as vacant on a periodic basis during the move operation

This method is practicable when the books constituting the minor
group are spread out in the classification and are not concentrated
in sets (which could be handled by blending or leaving specific sections vacant). Also, if the books are in another building or cannot
be handled as a blend, and there are enough of them so that whole
sections have to be designated for them, that too would indicate
the use of Method 4.

The technique of designating sections to be vacant on a periodic
basis would have been a proper choice in the National Library of
Medicine move with respect to the quartos and octavos of the 20th
Century monograph collection, if it had not been possible to accomplish the union of the major and minor groups prior to the move.
The facts in the NLM situation were such that both the octavos
(major group) and the quartos (minor group) covered the NLM "W"
classification and there were no large sets which could have fitted
in by blending or by leaving sections vacant. Returning to the NLM
data we find that there was a total of 8,251 linear feet of books,
octavos and quartos combined. The octavos aggregated 6,619 linear
feet and the quartos 1,632 linear feet. Since only 10 linear feet
were assigned to each section in the new building, this would mean
allocating 662 sections for the octavos and 163 sections for the
quartos. The octavos (major group) would be moved first, with
certain Sections being designated on a periodic basis to be left

vacant (to receive the quartos which would come in later and be
fitted in).

The quartos and the octavos (together) would require a total of
825 sections. To determine what sections we would leave vacant to
receive the quartos we divide 825 sections by 163 sections:

$$\frac{825}{163} = 5.06.$$ Thus, every fifth section would be left vacant. This would provide us with 165 vacant sections $\left(\frac{825}{5} = 165\right)$.

The disadvantage of this system is that it is an approximation.
Leaving every "i"th section vacant means that the incoming material has to be fitted in, involving some shifting. The shifting, is
however, more easily accomplished (there is simply more space to
maneuver in than in Method 1. Merging, prior to the move (Method
1) has the virtue of getting as much of the work as possible accomplished before the move.

Method 1 may not be practicable in some cases. In the UCLA
move of the Institute of Industrial Relations Library Methods 3
and 4 were used. This was simply because this library's material
was of two kinds; it was heavily concentrated in certain areas of
the classification (large sets) so as to make Method 3 (reserving
specific sections) feasible. There was also material which was
spread out to a larger degree. Here Method 4 was utilized and
periodic sections were reserved to have the material come in later.

Method 5: Merger following the main move

Under this method the major group is moved to the new building
first with the minor group following. No additional sections are
reserved to receive the minor group but it is counted in the total
space for that class. Basically, this method is a shelving operation. The characteristics which render this a practicable procedure
are: the material is spread out over the entire LC classification;
it does not bunch up at any one point in the classification enough to
make it convenient to reserve Sections; it is so located that "blending" is impracticable. Essentially, it applies to small groups of
materials as compared with the major group, and in summary, is
a relatively easy shelving job after the basic group has been moved.

"Very small" can be made more specific by relating the UCLA major groups to the minor groups in the Graduate Reserve Room collection for selected LC classes.

Table 12

Comparison of Graduate Reading Room Collection with Main collection, UCLA Library

LC Class	Major group	Minor group
A	5514	40
B	3777	67
C	652	77
D	9480	76

The minor group from inspection of Table 12, is very small and can properly be regarded as a shelving job after the major group has been moved.

Method 5 can be used conveniently in conjunction with Method 3 (whereby we leave specific sections vacant). This is precisely the combination used for the Graduate Reading Room Collection. The size of the GRR collection is shown in Table 13. It will be noted that it aggregates 1,052 linear feet, spread out over the entire LC classification, with two bulges at H and at P. Further check indicated sets in excess of 5 linear feet; this is shown as Table 14. Here Method 3 was utilized and specific sections were designated to remain vacant.

Some conclusions on mergers

As a general rule it is desirable to complete mergers before the move. Among other things, it eliminates complicating factors during the course. However, it may not be practicable for a number of reasons to execute a merger procedure prior to the move. In such cases, the other methods described or a combination of them set forth may be of assistance.

Table 13

Measurement of books in the Graduate Reading Room, UCLA
Library

Class	Linear feet
A	40
B	67
C	7
D	76
E	18
F	5
G	9
H	333
J	45
K	3
L	116
M	-
N	3
P	242
Q	5
R	37
S	1
T	2
U	-
V	1
X	-
Z	42
TOTAL	1052

It is necessary to have two measurements . First, we need a
measurement by sub-class of all the book materials in all minor
groups going into the new building shelves. Secondly, we need an
inventory within the first measurement, of all sets occupying more
than a specified number of linear feet. These data are needed to
plan the type of merger or combination of mergers which will be
necessary.

Table 14

Inventory of sets and decision on number of empty Sections
Graduate Reading Room, UCLA Library
(Sets 5 lin. ft. and over)

Call Number	Linear Feet
DC130 S2A3 1879	6
F592 T42	6
F851 B22	7
HQ1 J82	6
HV1 S67	7
HV1 S95	12
HV2510 A51	10
HV741 U58	8
HV88 N21	12
PB6 M72	15
PQ2070 1785	7
PQ2070 1877	6
PQ2084 1985	7
PQ2435 A1	5
PR5251 C77	6
RA790 M52	9
Z921 J61b	7
TOTAL	136

Study of the reference collection in the reading
rooms

The collections of reference materials, and plans for their expansion, should be studied and plans for development. Perhaps the
collection is to be expanded in the new building, or it may be decided that the collection will remain basically the same size as at
present. It is probably unlikely that the collection will be reduced
in size except for weeding. However, if a change either upward or
downward is contemplated, additional work is in order. A decrease
in the size of the reference collection, for example, should lead to
a program for returning volumes to the main collections in accordance with a time schedule and if possible, well before the main
stack collection is measured.

If an increase in the size of the reference collection is contemplated before the move, it is important to determine space possibilities for such expansion. In most instances, however, the increase in the size of the reference collection would occur over a
period of time and take place in the new building environment.
Hence, the best "cushion" for growth is to place the present collection into the new reference shelves in the new building at a uniform
liberal "stacking formula".

The actual measurement of the reference collection can be done
by the sampling procedures already described; alternatively, a
direct count can be made. Both of these should be in terms of
linear feet. If under 100 shelves are involved it may be desirable
to measure all of these in terms of linear feet of shelf displacement; a total higher than 100 shelves should probably be handled
by sampling.

The NLM and UCLA plans adopted the theory that the reference
collection would reflect current needs of clientele, and that weeding and addition would be a continuous process both before and after
the move. Thus, additions would cancel out retirements from the
collection. No large-scale changes were made regarding the size of
the reference collections in either move.

The more difficult aspect of measurement, however, in connection with the reference collections in reading rooms is not so much

the books on shelves but rather the index, directories, and dic-
tionaries which are shelved on special furniture and tables. Here
the planning has to deal with individual indexes and measurements
related to the new building environment. Enlarged copies of the
floor plans showing the new building tables, desks, etc. are of
enormous help in marking the prospective location of reference tools
of this category.

The card catalogs

The catalog card cabinets for the public card catalog, the shelf
list and auxiliary files in the present building may be intended for
transfer to the new building, that is, no new cabinets may be provided. This, then, is a move problem concerned solely with the
physical transfer of the cabinets and their placement in new quarters.

Alternatively, new cabinets may be provided to house the public
catalog and also the shelf list in the new building. If the number of
new cabinets and trays match the number existing in the present
building, we are faced with a problem of the physical transfer of
the cabinets and the shifting of the cards to the new cabinets and
trays. (Here we have a replacement of the furniture by no additional cabinets.) The number of cards per tray may be adequate and a
simple transfer of cards from old to new trays is required.

However, when a library is involved in a move, it is likely that
the present trays and cabinets are crowded and that the new cabinets provide substantially more capacity than does the present
equipment.

We will need a finding as to the number of catalog cards in the
various catalogs (public card catalog, shelflist, etc.), the number
of trays and their dimensions, the average percentage to which the
trays are filled, the growth rate, and the number of trays in the
new catalog cabinets in the new building.

It is very likely that in planning the new building, specifically
for the card catalog cabinets and trays that a survey of the present card catalog and future requirements has been conducted. These
data should be secured and studied; they can probably form the ba-

sis of the count of catalog cards. With a determinant number of
catalog cards and a determinant number of new trays in the new
building we have established the number of cards to be placed in
each new tray. One consideration involved is the number and location of empty trays (for long-term expansion purposes).

The total number of non-empty card trays should be determined
by inspection of the card catalog; concurrently, the record should
show the interior capacity of the trays. The trays may be of 15"
or 18" capacity (or some other size) or a combination of different
sizes. Multiplying the total number of non-empty trays by the linear
inch capacity will produce total linear inches of catalog card tray
space. If some trays are of 15" capacity and others of 18" capacity,
it will, of course, be necessary to multiply the number of 15" trays
by the number of trays with this dimension, and the number of 18"
trays by the number of trays of this dimension. The addition of
these two products will produce total linear inches of non-empty
catalog card tray space.

(Number of Non-empty Trays + (Number of Non-empty   Total Inches
of 15 Inch Length X 15"   Trays of 18 Inch Length = of Non-
                              X 18"   Empty Cata-
                                                         log Tray
                                                         Space.

Measurement of the catalog cards

Consideration should be given to sampling the non-empty trays to
determine linear inches of cards in the trays. This can avoid heavy
expense in measuring the contents of hundreds of trays on an individual basis. The services of a statistician should be sought before making any of the sample measurements since the sample size
will have to be determined and we will want to know range or variation in the number of inches of cards from tray to tray and the
relative accuracy required in our final measurement. The number
of linear inches of cards in each sample tray should be recorded on
a tally sheet displayed as a Move Planning Form (Figure 11). In the
measuring process the cards should be pressed together tightly and
the linear inches of cards recorded in multiples of quarter inches.
The beginning of the "systematic sample" should be based on a be-

Figure 11

Move Planning Form

Sampling tally sheet for the measurement of catalog cards

| Date samples taken: | Population (number of non-empty catalog card trays): |
| Interior length of catalog card trays: | Sample size (number of non-empty catalog card trays sampled: |

Tally

Designation of tray number	Sample tray:	Linear inches of catalog cards recorded decimally in quarter inch multiples
	1	
	2	
	3	
	4	
	5	
	6	
	7	
	8	
	9	
	0	
Sub-total		
Arithmetic mean		

ginning tray selected at random. To select a sample of 300 trays from a population of 3,000, the first step, with this design, would be to divide 3,000 by 300 to obtain a "sampling interval", here 10. Next, a random number should be selected (between 01 and 10). If this number turns out to be 5, then the start should be at the 5th tray and every 10th tray should be inspected thereafter until the full 300 trays in the sample have been recorded.

The arithmetic mean of the 300 samples is the figure to be

multiplied by the number of non-empty catalog card trays. (The
measurement is best retained in linear inches.) Thus,

$$\text{Arithmetic mean X } \frac{\text{Population of Non-empty}}{\text{Catalog Card Trays}} = \frac{\text{Linear Inches of}}{\text{Catalog Cards}}$$

We can secure the number of cards by multiplying by a constant
factor (the number of cards per linear inch).

Whether or not sampling is utilized the presentation of the figures is probably best set out in terms of the catalog card trays in
a section of the present building cabinets (which may hold, say, 12
trays). Thus, if all trays were measured in multiples of quarter
inches, we would then have a sub-total of linear inches of cards for
the section. If sampling were used we would have an estimated total
of linear inches of cards. In either case, we would have a series
of sub-totals, in linear inches, of the cards by section and of
course, the grand total.

If we divide our grand total of linear inches of cards either the
actual total or the estimated total (if we use a sample) by the
number of new trays in the new cabinets we intend to use in the
new building, we have the average tray occupancy in linear inches
for the new trays. (We may not intend to use all the trays in the
new babinets, preferring to keep some in reserve.)

The sub-total for the first 12 tray section in our present cabinets may, for example, be 180 inches of catalog cards. The end
of this increment of 180 inches of cards may be termed a "control
point," that is, we will use it to check the reliability of our total
measurement. The end of each increment of cards in each of the
remaining sections of 12 trays each also represent control points.
If we assume that in our new trays the average occupancy is to be
9 inches then we should expect that 20 new trays will be required
(180 inches divided by the 9 inch average). This figure of 9 inches
is, of course, derived from our measurement of the linear inches
of cards in all the trays (or the estimated total linear inches by
sampling procedures) divided by the number of new trays we intend
to use in the new cabinets.

Now if this figure is relatively accurate we should find, if we
measure off increments of 9 inches each, beginning with the first

tray, that we should have a series of exactly 20 increments when
we finish the first section of 12 trays. This is the significance of
the "control point".

It is convenient to have a chart illustrating the number and type
of arrangement of the new catalog card cabinet (Figure 12). Each
box represents a tray and can be numbered; we can indicate on
this chart in which tray the control point occurs, and also at what
point in the new tray-to-be (whether 1/4, 1/2, 3/4, or end of the
new tray-to-be. In the example used, we have 180 inches of cards
for our present first section of 12 trays. The 180 inches divided
by 9 average inches for the new tray works out to 20 trays of the
new catalog. Thus, tray 20 on the chart would be marked "End" to
show that the control point comes at the end of new tray Number
20. (The second half of the label for the present section is also
recorded in the box.) If we have, for example, 168.5 inches in our
second group of 12 tray sections then we would divide 168.5 by 9
inches to secure 18.7 new trays. On our chart we would indicate at
new tray number 39 (having used the first 20), "3/4" and the second half of the label.

How closely the control point is reached is relative and must
take into account the extent of the catalog card tray being moved.
The preferred measurement is the one indicating the 9 inch increments, however, if this departs from the control point we face the
possibility of ending up with more cards than new trays or con-
versely, a number of completely empty trays at the end of the
cabinet. Guide cards will have to be prepared for insertion into the
present card catalog trays at the 9 inch increments (in this example).
These colored guide cards, to indicate the new sub-division, will
be consecutively numbered to agree with the total of new trays in
the new cabinets. By inserting these in the present trays at the
intervals designated we can test the accuracy of the control points.
Complete agreement with the control point is not necessarily desirable since we may want to make a break from tray to tray that is
logical. Thus, the testing of the control point by the insertion of
the numbered guide cards is practicable. One other factor bears

Figure 12
DIAGRAM OF NEW CARD CATALOG CABINET
AND INDICATION OF CONTROL POINTS

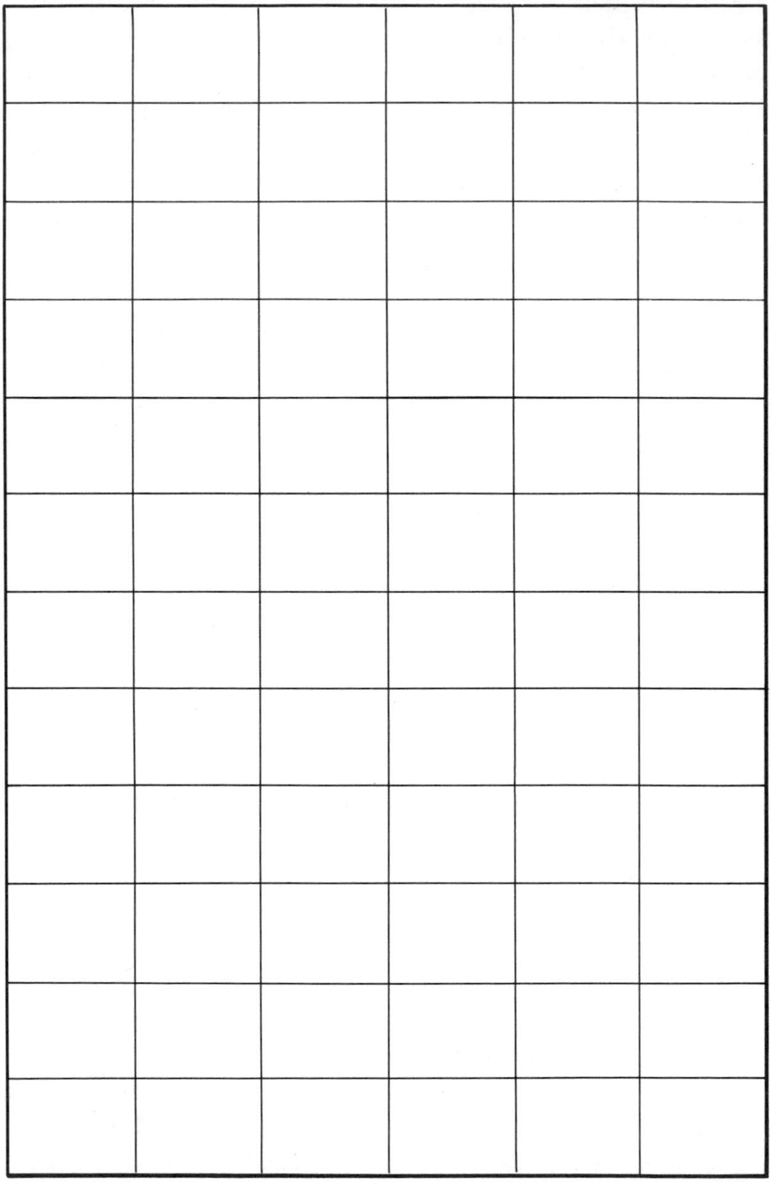

mention. In placing the numbered guide cards at intervals of 9 inches we must be careful to designate those guide cards which represent trays which will not be occupied (perhaps the entire bottom row of the new cabinets).

This can be done by placing the numbered guide card in the old tray but marking it "Empty" and not allowing the 9 inches of cards to be placed after it. (If, for example, tray 4236 in the new cabinets is to be empty, the guide card with "4236" would be marked "Empty tray" and there would follow, in the old tray, the guide card 4237 with 9 inches of cards after it.)

Growth of the card catalog

Figures may exist in the library as to the number of cards per title or number of cards per volume. The importance of such a figure is that it can be used in conjunction with the anticipated growth of the book collections to estimate the future growth of the card catalog.

If figures are not available on number of cards per title (or volume) then they can be worked out in approximate fashion by using the total linear inches of catalog cards, comparing this figure with the number of titles or volumes reported in the library statistics. This has to be done with some caution. For example, the card catalog may contain the cards for branch libraries as well; the growth rate for books might be based perhaps on the main library only so the growth rate for the card catalog might be greater than that for the main library book collection.

To recapitulate we would have total linear inches of cards multiplied by 100 cards per inch (or by the constant found to be most accurate in a given library situation). This will produce the figure of total cards on hand. The ratio of cards to titles (or volumes) can be obtained by securing the comparable year's count of titles or volumes in the collections. Thus,

$$\frac{\text{Total cards}}{\text{Total titles (or vols.)}} = \text{Cards per title (or volume)}$$

The significance of this is that the projected added titles or volumes can be multiplied by the ratio of cards per title or volume to get an idea of the size of the card catalog in the years ahead.

The UCLA Library figures (Table 15) illustrate the relationship between volumes and titles on one hand and cards on the other hand.

Table 15

Cards per title and cards per volume produced for the Public
Catalog, UCLA Library, for the period FY 1956 - 1962

Year	Titles	Volumes	Cards Added to Catalog	Cards per Title	Cards per Volume
1955/56	38,382	71,558	101,211	2.6	1.4
1956/57	38,207	62,179	91,572	2.4	1.5
1957/58	35,667	70,528	100,627	2.8	1.4
1958/59	35,307	75,512	110,760	3.1	1.2
1959/60	39,295	75,980	113,302	2.8	1.4
1960/61	41,499	75,253	165,645	3.9	2.2
1961/62	40,024	81,624	144,600	3.6	1.7
Totals	268,381	512,634	827,717	3.1	1.6

Note: The cards per title and cards per volume are rounded off to the first decimal so these estimates will be approximations; but they will be close enough for all practical purposes.

Providing growth space in the card catalog

All trays can be filled at a relatively low rate of occupancy in the new building in order to provide for growth. On the other hand, a certain number of trays may be filled to moderate density with adjacent trays above and below being left vacant. The latter procedure creates layers, both above and below the card trays used. Figures 13 and 14 illustrates these alternatives. Nine inches, in general, of cards per 18 inch tray, with some trays left completely vacant, is a desirable beginning occupancy ratio.

Preparation for moving the card catalog

The present cabinets may be scheduled for use in the new building. A careful examination should be made of the cabinets to ascertain the possibility of moving the cabinets with the trays remain-

Figure 13

NATIONAL LIBRARY OF MEDICINE
PUBLIC CARD CATALOG CABINET

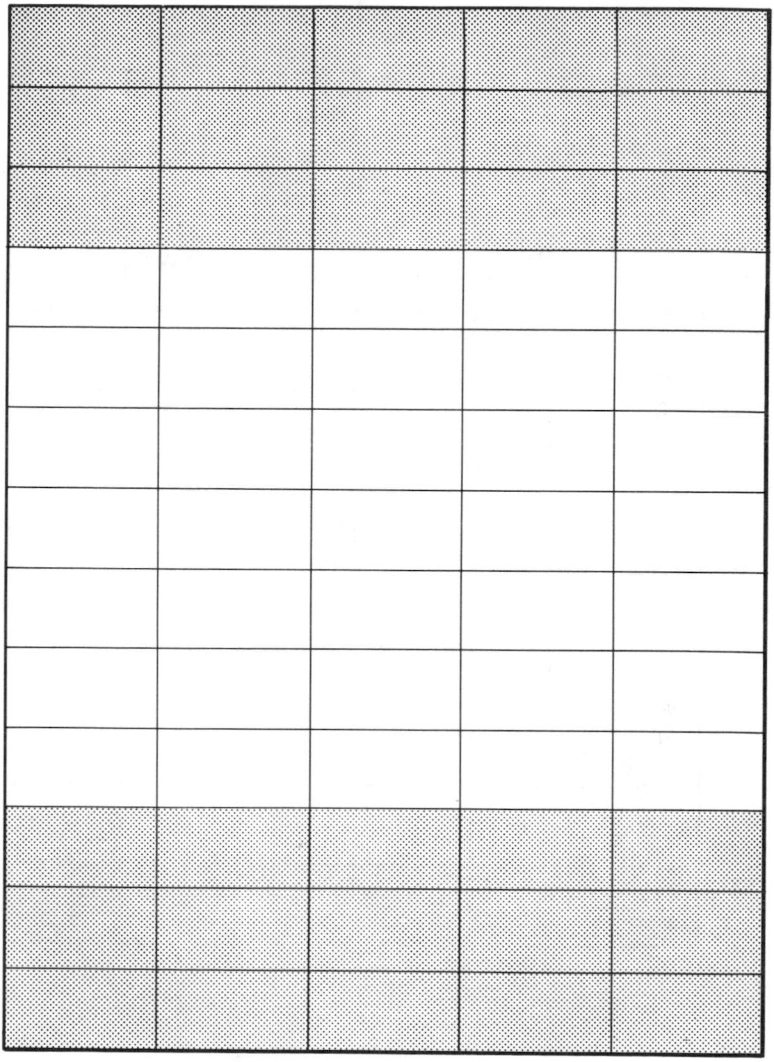

70 cabinets, 65 trays each, 4550 trays total
13 trays high, 5 trays wide
30 trays vacant each cabinet (shaded)

95

Figure 14
UCLA LABRARY
PUBLIC CARD CATALOG CABINET

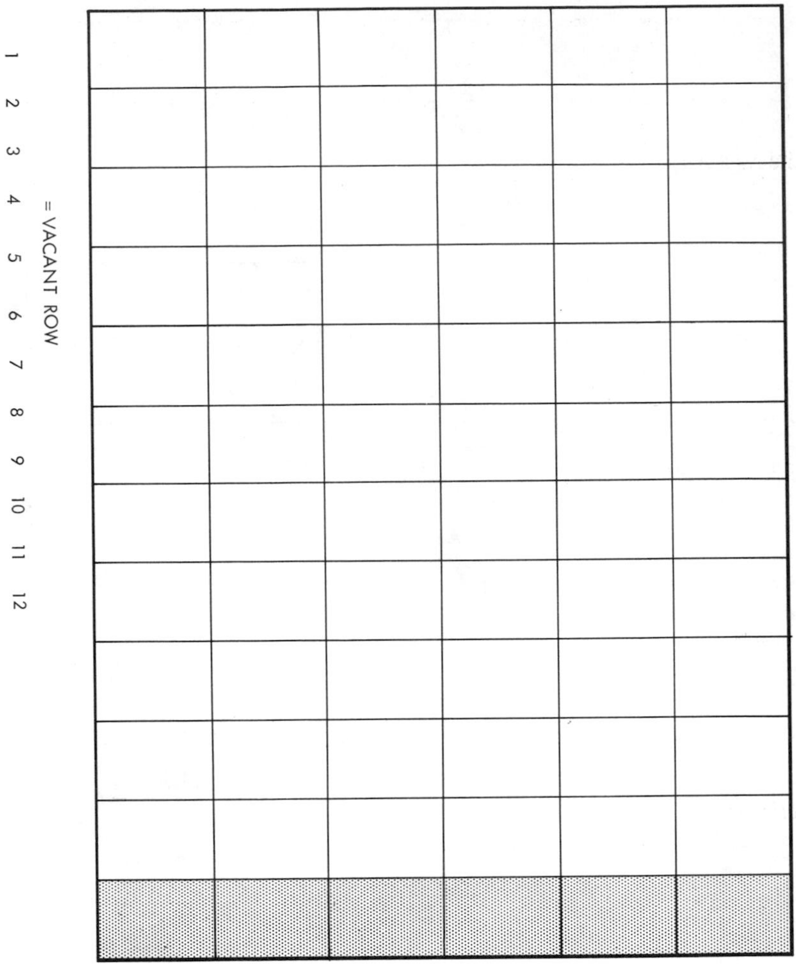

= VACANT ROW

67 cabinets, 72 trays each, 4,824 trays total

12 trays high, 6 trays wide

6 trays vacant each cabinet. (shaded)

ing in the cabinets. Especial attention should be given the nature of
the construction and the relative deterioration in the adhesive join-
ing the cabinet parts. The cabinets may be composed of relatively
small independent sections, permitting moving without removal of
the trays. Even if the cabinets are large, it is still possible to
move them as a unit by use of a dolly. The mover should, however, be consulted as to feasibility of moving the trays in their
cabinets.

Even if the present cabinets are not to be used in the new building, it is desirable to consider moving the cabinets as containers
for the trays if this is feasible. In the NLM move some cabinets
were moved as containers; in other instances the cabinets were
too weak and the trays were placed in large wooden boxes. In the
UCLA move the public catalog cabinets could not be used as containers because of their size. The shelf-list, however, was in
smaller units and the move was made with the trays in the cabinets.
In all instances where the cabinets are moved with the trays in the
cabinet, masking tape (one or two inch masking tape) should be
used completely around the cabinet to hold the trays in place.

The preparation of the card trays for moving should include
compressing the cards toward the front of the tray.

When the trays cannot be moved in the cabinet there are several
other methods available. Large wooden boxes were used in the
NLM move; each box contained about 12 trays, in two layers of
six trays each. A piece of plywood separated the two layers. In
the UCLA move large bindery boxes were used to advantage. Here
a total of 8 18-inch trays were moved, in two layers of four trays.
This method was utilized for some 3,000 public card catalog trays.

An alternative procedure, in consultation with the mover is to
wind a special plastic tape around trays mounted on a dolly with
layers of plywood separating the layers of trays. The number of
trays and the size of the dolly has to be studied with care. Elevator exits, narrow aisles, etc. in the present and new buildings
will affect the size of the package placed on the dolly. This method accelerates the moving of card trays from the present to the

new building.

Study of work in progress

The move director should examine the work in progress throughout the library some months before actual move time in order to
identify potential problem areas. The time lapse for moving a given
department is partly determined by the amount of material it has
on hand for processing. A review of this sort can lead to reducing
the amount of material to be moved. For example, material ready
for the bindery should be sent out before move time; or they may
be left in the old building for pick-up. Exchange materials have
been discussed. As move day approaches it will probably be desirable not to open routine shipments from bookdealers; the books can
be moved in their original packages or stored in the new building
shipping area under proper control.

Books in process of cataloging need measurement to secure an
idea of the number of booktrucks necessary. The assignment of
numbers of volumes to individual catalogers should be reduced as
move time approaches; the number of small moves, individual booktrucks, directed to individual work stations is to be minimized.
The material in process can be moved with greater ease if concentrated.

The examples cited are typical of a number of situations which,
if identified and provided for, can increase the efficiency of the
move. Work in progress requires review. Failure to note the nature and magnitude of the work in progress can upset the move
schedule.

Work in progress in cataloging and acquisition can be moved on
booktrucks, with wooden boxes to take care of microfilms; this
means planning for a suitable number of booktrucks for the period
of such a move.

A supply of cardboard containers, approximately 20" x 18" x 12",
should be on hand well before moving time. A ratio of 2 boxes for
each staff member is probably ample. The boxes can be re-used
during the move since the different departments will be moved at
different times. Such containers are for in-desk and on-desk ma-

terials. Each box should bear the name of the staff member and
his room number or level in the new building, inscribed clearly.

Such boxes should be distributed to staff members at the right
time; too early will preclude continued production, making them
available too late will involve haste and confusion. A day before
actual move time is satisfactory.

A wooden box should be used for the contents of supply cabinets.
Steel correspondence file cabinets, on the contrary, need not be
emptied; the correspondence can be packed tight and moved in its
cabinet. In both the National Library of Medicine and UCLA moves
the correspondence file cabinets were used as move cartons and
contents transferred by staff members in the new building to the
new cabinets.

Desk reference books, or reference materials in proximity to
the desks, may be best handled on booktrucks which should bear a
placard indicating name of staff member (or work station) and floor
and room designation. Such placards, of heavy cardboard (one per
booktruck), should be about 10" x 14" and can be lettered with a
fluid marking pencil.

Notes

1. The Thesis Collection at the National Library of Medicine provides a number of interesting commentaries on the questions reviewed here. First, the terminology of "volumes" may, in fact, be
"pieces". According to the 1960 NLM Annual Report the Thesis Collection numbered 284,882 pieces and the total collections of the Library aggregated 1,084,256 "pieces". In this context, then, the
Thesis Collection constituted 26 percent of the total collections.
However, in terms of shelf displacement, the linear feet of shelf
space consumed by this collection was on the order of 3,000 linear
feet; the total collections of the NLM turned out to be 65,000 linear
feet. Thus, the Thesis Collection represented some 5 percent of the
total collections in this context.
    The volume of "piece" count here portrayed is interesting in
another aspect when compared to the actual shelf displacement.
Much of the Thesis collection was not composed of bound volumes but
individual theses were stored in metal boxes and the arrangement of
the theses within the boxes was from front-to-back rather than in the
usual left-to-right sequence, again stressing the importance of shelf
displacement in terms of linear feet as standard.

Chapter 4

The New Building Environment

Purpose

The new building should be studied first as a physical structure
---its design, location of offices, reading rooms, bookstacks, elevators, loading platforms, etc. All these factors affect the moving
operation as well as proper functioning of the new building. We
are concerned, accordingly, not only with moving from the present
building to the new building, but also with the right arrangement of
the new building's contents.

The new building is also examined with reference to the furniture and equipment that will be placed in it. This includes the used
furniture and equipment which will be moved to the new building
from the present building, and the new furniture and equipment
which will be delivered directly to the new building by the contractor. Finally, the new building is studied with reference to the many
factors involved in its receiving and housing the collections of library materials. This last approach will occupy the major
portion of our attention in this chapter.

The distribution, location, and capacity of the bookstack areas
in terms of ranges, sections, shelves, and capacity in linear feet
will be covered. The concept "section" is fundamental in the development of the data, more so than measurement in terms of "range,"
"shelf," or "linear feet."

The assignment of individual collections to specific areas will be
discussed and the relative value of certain areas will be treated. Another concern will be the "stacking formula" or the percent by which we
fill the sections with book materials in order to provide for growth.

The present chapter is a continuation of the material presented
in Chapter 3, where the magnitude, characteristics, and growth
trends of the various collections were established. In the present
chapter we are concerned with the utilization of these data in the

100

logistics of placing the materials in the new building. Possible improvements in the arrangement of the collections should be kept in
mind in reviewing the various alternatives for placing the collections in the new building.

Status of new building construction

It is assumed, for purposes of this text, that the new building is
in the course of construction and that the location and amount of
space assigned to the various departments have already been decided. The precise status of the new building construction at the
time we begin the move planning is important. A comprehensive
inspection should be made of the new building in conjunction with
review of the building schedule. Preferably, this is done in con-
ference with the person responsible for construction.

The actual state of construction should be checked against the
schedule in order that variations be determined and a new forecast obtained. Among the important progress points to be checked
at the beginning of move planning and periodically thereafter are:
electrical system, telephone circuits and placement of instruments,
air conditioning system, procurement and placement of new furniture and equipment, catalog cabinets, and placement of book shelving
in the bookstacks. A list of the various elements requiring completion will indicate the various elements or operations which are
in progress. This list should have space to indicate progress at a
given time, the scheduled date for completion, and space for anno-
tations. The purpose of this exercise is to have all of the necessary
elements brought together at a certain time which we might describe
simply as new building readiness. This is the date toward which we
will be working and the date which will determine when the actual
moving may begin and the date on which we expect to make the
new building the center of library activities.

Part of the planning consists in preparing a floor layout for
each of the floors of the new building, using a set of the floor
plans. Such layouts fulfill a number of important functions, such
as indicating to the movers the location of various work stations
and the destination of equipment or material. A floor plan is of

use, too, in orienting staff members to the new building and
familiarizing them with it.

New and used furniture can be conveniently distinguished on the
floor layouts by shading the used furniture on the plans: furniture
may be further designated by writing in the property or serial
number on the layout. One set of floor plans may be used to designate a special position number which refers to each work station
(desk) in the new building. This number will then be used by the
staff member to identify the material going to his desk at the time
of the move.

If the location of the furniture and equipment has not already
been decided upon, it is a good idea to employ the Chart-Pak
technique or similar technique to help work out the space problems. (The Chart-Pak system consists of a large grid and a supply of scaled templates to represent walls, desks, files, chairs,
etc.)

It is a good idea to check the kind of work to be performed at
a given location to make certain that the proper auxiliary units
have been ordered, that is, typist table, office machines, etc.
In positioning new furniture and equipment it is advisable to flow-
chart the work processes for each work unit. The arrangement
of furniture in relation to the underfloor ducts should also be
checked.

The Bookstack Areas: designation and labelling

We will want to examine the bookstacks, their characteristics,
their number, and relation to elevators and to the booklifts serving
circulation desks in the reading rooms. It is necessary to examine
the new building floor layout with reference to aisles and possible
routes from the loading platform to the various stack areas. In
addition, the placement of the collections of library materials in
the new bookstack areas must be studied with respect to the principles involved, provision for growth and other relevant matters.

An accurate layout of the bookstack areas, illustrating all of
the floors to contain shelving, is indispensable. It is vitally important to make a thorough examination of the bookstack areas and

the actual bookstacks as they are being erected in order to ensure
conformity of the placement with the plans. It is well to have the
floor layouts suitably enlarged, in several copies, for drafting and
other operating purposes. A fluid marking pencil for sketching in
the names and numbers of the various parts of the bookstack areas,
the sequence of shelving, and the route(s) to be followed in the
movement of the books into the new bookstack areas is desirable.
Figure 15 indicates one of the main bookstack areas of the new
National Library of Medicine building as an example; this is Level
A, partly devoted to office space and partly to bookstacks. The
chart has also been marked to indicate the route followed in the
moving operation. The loading platform is situated at the south end
of Level A marking the use of elevator in this part of the move.
Level B, beneath Level A, is illustrated in Figure 16.

On a suitably enlarged (photostat) reproduction of the various
levels or floors, the areas or clusters of bookstacks should be
identified by means of letters and/or numbers. For example, the
topmost floor or level might be designated by the letter "A", the
second, "B", etc. The letter designations for floors can then be
suffixed by numbers. This is illustrated for Level B in the new
National Library of Medicine building (Figure 16). The designations ought to be made with one side of the building serving as
the starting point. Actually, any logical system of designation will
be suitable, the main point being to have a "name" or reference
point for each area for simple vocabulary and identification purposes.

Capacity of the new bookstack Areas

We can ascertain the capacity of the various areas in the new
building in terms of the number of sections and linear feet of
shelving we will have on hand for use.

This is not strictly accurate because the capacity of the bookstack areas is dependent upon the number of shelves we incorpor-
ate in the sections. Normally, this will be a total of seven (base
shelf and six movable) shelves, giving us a capacity of 21 linear
feet per section. The difficulty is imposed by the fact, that in

Figure 15

Moving route, National Library of Medicine building (Level A)

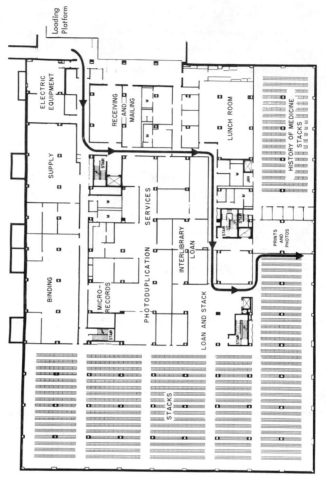

NATIONAL LIBRARY OF MEDICINE

R.B. O'Connor & W.H. Kilham Jr.   Architects

"A" LEVEL

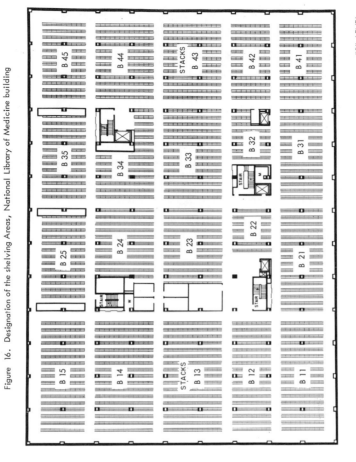

Figure 16

Figure 16. Designation of the shelving Areas, National Library of Medicine building

"B" LEVEL

NATIONAL LIBRARY OF MEDICINE
R.B. O'Connor & W.H. Kilham Jr. Architects

105

some instances, we may utilize a total of six shelves (base and
five adjustable) for certain kinds of materials, such as large
quartos, government documents, etc., thus yielding 18 linear feet
of shelving per section. Thus, until we have determined the nature
of the collections with respect to the heights of books we cannot
make a definitive statement of the capacity of the bookstack areas
in the new building.

Since the number of shelves per section will determine the
capacity of the new bookstacks the space to be left between shelves
will be discussed first. A 90 inch upright with seven shelves is
most common. In some instances the library will have a 96 inch
upright, providing for up to eight shelves. In the new NLM building the 96 inch uprights were fitted with a base and six movable
shelves. It was planned to add a shelf when necessary, where
height of the volumes will permit. In the new UCLA Library 90
inch uprights were installed except in one area on each of three
floors (120 sections each), which had 96 inch uprights. This shelving was intended for oversize volumes.

The amount of space to be allowed between the shelves is
dependent upon the height of the books to be placed in the section.
In most instances, this will provide seven shelves. For oversize
books a base shelf and five adjustable shelves will probably be
normal. Given the number of shelves per section, shelves may be
spaced in a variety of ways but are normally spaced uniformly. On
a 90 inch upright with a base shelf and six adjustable shelves the
standard spacing may be carried out in a number of ways. These
are illustrated in Figure 17.

The spacing for 90 inch uprights with seven shelves will range
from 10 to 12 inches. The choice will be dictated by the height
of the material and, to some extent, by the desire to have the
top shelf as short a distance from the floor as possible.

A 96 inch upright provides somewhat greater latitude but the
spacing should be based on the nature of the material rather than
the availability of the extra six inches. Extending the spacing would
make the top or seventh shelf quite high and would hinder the addi-

Figure 17
SPACING BETWEEN SHELVES ON
90 INCH UPRIGHT

Inches of clear space between shelves; distance from floor to top of each shelf shown in cumulated inches	10 inch clear space between shelves *	11 inch clear space between shelves	12 inch clear space between shelves	13 inch clear space between shelves

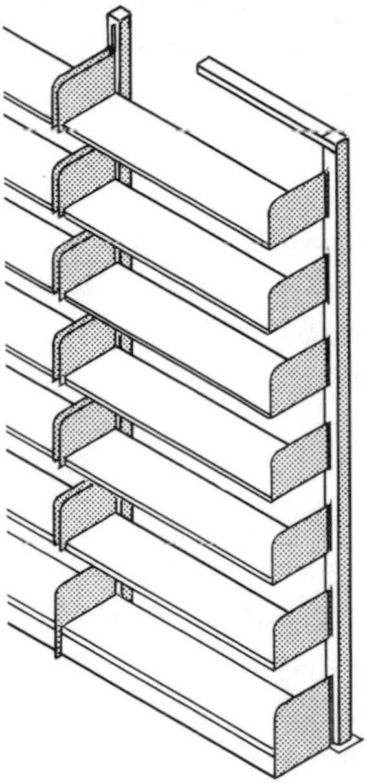

{ 90 inch mark
Distance between top shelf and 90 inch line representing top or upright

	14.25	8.25	2.25
	73.75	81.75	87.75
	64.00	69.00	74.00
	52.25	56.25	60.25
	40.50	43.50	46.50
	28.75	30.75	32.75
	17.00	18.00	19.00
	5.25	5.25	5.25

Base plate computed at 5.25 inches, i.e., 5.25 inches from

top of base shelf to floor;

Thickness of each shelf computed at 0.75 inches.

107

tion of an eighth shelf in the future.

Within the limits imposed by the fact that we have six adjustable shelves for standard spacing on either 90 or 96 inch uprights, we must take into account the nature of the material, and select that spacing which will suffice to take care of a very high percentage, say 95 percent, of the books, with individual shelf adjustment being made on an ad hoc basis during the course of the move. The top shelf should be as close to the floor as possible, not only to permit easier reaching of the book but also to make possible the addition of an eighth shelf in the future without shifting.

It is probably desirable to set the spacing at the maximum possible on a uniform basis, namely 12 clear inches. This avoids the manipulation of shelves in the move operation as far as possible.

In Figure 17 we assume that the base shelf is 5.25 inches from the floor. (This will vary from library to library.) It is assumed also that there are 6 adjustable shelves each 0.75 inches in thickness. There is then a total of 9.75 inches taken up before we allocate distance between shelves. If we decide upon 11.00 inches between shelves then we have 11.00 x 6 adjustable shelves or 66.00. To this is added the 9.75 inches for a total of 75.75 inches, which is the distance from the top shelf to the floor.

A spacing of 13 inches between shelves will not normally be possible on a 90 inch upright, given the 5.25 inch base.

If the bottom or base shelf is to be left vacant for expansion, then the space between the base shelf and the first movable shelf can be reduced somewhat, perhaps to 8 or 9 inches. This simply means that the topmost shelf is a bit more reachable (to the extent that the first movable shelf is lowered). This procedure was adopted in the new NLM building.

On the other hand, the new UCLA building was set up with uniform spacing between shelves so that the bottom shelf, to take care of rapid growth, would be readily available with no adjustment of shelves.

The stack contractor ordinarily places the shelves on the stack uprights. This placement might just as well be done on the basis

Table 16

Distance Between Shelves With Differing Number of Shelves Per Section and Height Of Shelves From Floor

Height of Upright		90"	90"	90"	90"	96"	96"	96"	96"
No. of shelves		7	6	5	4	7	6	5	4
Space between shelves (inches)		12.00	14.00	18.00	24.00	13.00	14.00	18.00	24.00
Height of Shelves from floor (inches)	1*	5.25"	5.25	5.25	5.25	5.25	5.25	5.25	5.25
	2	18.00	20.00	24.00	30.00				
	3	30.75	34.75	42.75	54.75				
	4	43.50	49.50	61.50	79.50				
	5	56.25	64.25	80.25	-				-
	6	69.00	79.00	-	-			-	-
	7	81.75	-	-	-		-	-	-
Distance from top shelf to 90" level		8.25	11.00	9.75	10.50				

* Base computed at 4.50", with 0.75" shelf = 5.25"

of instructions from the library's move director, thus eliminating the work of changing the spacing.

Table 16 is a guide to distances between shelves when different number of shelves are used per section.

The capacity of the new areas should be determined fairly early. The stack drawings, labelled in accordance with the procedures already described, will form the basis of this determination. Most of the areas will have seven shelves. The areas that are to have six shelves should be noted if possible. While the interior dimension of shelves may range from 35.00 to 36.00 inches, the figure of 36 inches is adequate for all practical purposes.

For a given area on the stack drawings, count the number of sections in a single-faced range, then count the number of single-faced ranges. Multiply the number of sections per single-faced range by the number of single-faced ranges. This will give the total number of sections in the area except that the number of sections per range may not be constant because of the interposition of columns, so the number of sections lost because of columns must be deducted. This is why Figure 18 has a caption "sections deleted by columns." In addition, some areas may have ranges of different numbers of sections; this, again, will have to be noted in the tabulation.

The total number of sections can then be multiplied by the number of shelves per section, normally seven, giving us the total number of shelves in the area. The total number of shelves in the area can then be multiplied by the number of linear feet per shelf (3 feet) to obtain the total number of linear feet in the area.

It is the section, however, which is the unit in measurement and space allocation, rather than the number of shelves or linear feet, although these are of use and importance in other considerations.

Where tall volumes are expected to be shelved, the area may be outfitted with 6 shelves. The statement on capacity should reflect the fact that these sections have a capacity of 18 linear feet.

The importance of this is that when dealing with large volumes,

the sections have 6 shelves each and the actual capacity is 18
linear feet; if we place 10 linear feet of books in such a section
we have a section occupancy ratio of $\frac{10}{18}$ or 55.5 rather than the
more favorable $\frac{10}{21}$ or 47.6 Multiplied by a large number of sections this
difference is substantial. Thus, the decision to place this or that
number of linear feet of books into a particular section should take
cognizance of the section and its number of shelves.

It will be useful to tabulate these data according to area, total-
ing the areas to determine these figures according to stack levels
or floors, then adding the data for levels in order to secure the
grand total for the entire building. The figures for number of sections, shelves, and linear feet should also be superimposed on a
drawing of the stack plans, with the designation of area number.
A specimen of the tabulation of these data which may be followed
is illustrated in Figure 18.

The set of floor plans showing the bookstack areas should indicate the names or labels given the floors and the areas. As a
memory aid the drawings should have a record of the number of
sections, plus any other pertinent data. The stack drawings should
be mounted on a bulletin board or wall for easy consultation.

Calculation of the capacity of the bookstack areas does not end
here. These calculations provide the maximum capacity in areas,
ranges, sections, and in terms of linear feet of shelves; however,
it would be rare that shelves would be filled completely. When
newly acquired books are difficult to shelve at a given point in the
classification, difficult in the sense that some shifting is entailed,
other solutions such as major shifting is required or additional
library space must be sought. The practical or working capacity
is of the order of 75 to 80 percent of the theoretical capacity of
the shelves. Thus, an area with a theoretical capacity of 10,000
linear feet of shelving would have a practical capacity of 7,500 or
8,000 linear feet of shelving. The practical capacity, calculated on
the basis of 80 percent of the actual capacity, rounds out Figure 18.

This problem of practical capacity, while it is not a factor in
the move per se, is important in providing for growth of the col-

112

Figure 18

Move Planning Form

Inventory of sections, shelves and linear feet of shelving in the new library building.

Stack Floor _____

(1) Area name	(2) Number of single-faced ranges	(3) Number Sections per SF range	(4) Total Sections (col. 2 X col. 3)	(5) Sections deleted by columns	(6) Net total Sections (Col. 4 minus col. 5)	(7) Linear feet shelf space (col. 6 x 21 LF or constant factor)
Totals						

lections. It is in this latter context, discussed below, that the concept of practical capacity is a guide to the life expectancy of the bookstack areas. If 80 percent occupancy is considered the practical capacity the interval between 75 percent and 80 percent might be termed the critical interval.

Sequence in the arrangement of the collection

The order of shelving should be sketched on the stack plans. Normally, the collection will be shelved from left to right in each single faced range.

The sequence can be continuous as shown in Figure 19, illustrating the plan used in UCLA's University Research Library, or discontinuous as shown in Figure 15, illustrating Level A of the National Library of Medicine. In the latter arrangement, the beginning point in each area is in the same place.

Considerations in providing for growth

In considering the placement of an individual collection or a part of it in a specific area adequate provision must be made for estimated future growth based on past experience. It is not sufficient to know that Collection X comprises 5,000 linear feet and that the linear feet of the two areas to which this collection is assigned total 6,000 linear feet. Consideration must be given to space required for expansion. How do we take cognizance of the growth factor and make appropriate accommodation in the new bookstacks? The limiting factor is the number of sections or linear feet of shelving in the new building. There is a known number of linear feet of books to be placed in those sections. If the difference between the two is relatively small then the question of provision for growth is academic. On the other hand, if there is a substantial difference between the new building's capacity and the linear feet of books to be moved, then the consideration of growth takes on a different perspective, and the different collections or classifications are in competition for the growth space.

We may not have the past growth rate in terms of classification subdivisions in which case the total library growth rate would be used with the understanding, of course, that we are interested in the

Figure 19

SEQUENCE OF SHELVING

UCLA University
Research Library

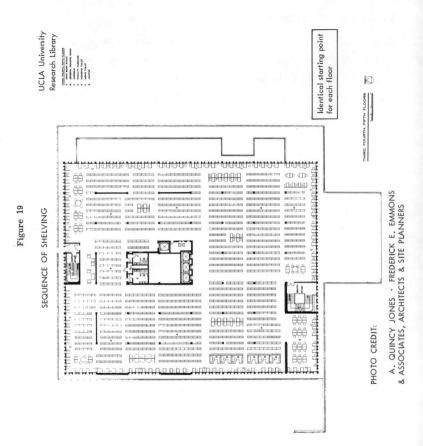

PHOTO CREDIT:

A. QUINCY JONES · FREDERICK E. EMMONS
& ASSOCIATES, ARCHITECTS & SITE PLANNERS

114

future growth rate and the estimate of future growth should determine the allocation of growth space in the new building.

Allocating growth space in the new building stack areas may be effected in a number of ways. Space can be left interspersed in various places or it may be left at the peripheral areas. Usually growth will occur throughout the classification, even though it may vary among individual libraries, growth space should be spread throughout the stack. Ideally it should anticipate unusual growth for certain classes. The precision with which we can pinpoint future growth leaves something to be desired.

In the mechanics of moving it is essential to provide growth space on a systematic, standardized, basis. This does not mean that the identical formula has to be used for all subject classes. The provision of space for growth should exist on the individual shelf, which should be partly empty; in the section, where one or two shelves should be empty; and empty sections should be spaced throughout the stack floor.

The amount of space left empty in the section, and the entirely empty sections, can be varied according to estimated growth needs. If growth needs are not known or are doubtful the best possible reserve for expansion is systematic provision of free space. In fact, the provision of growth space can be viewed as creating a pattern of pockets of free space throughout the new bookstack areas.

The decision to provide uniform growth space throughout has some disadvantages. Some empty spaces will be filled more slowly than others; however, even distribution of growth space means that only minor shifting will be required to use the uniformly distributed expansion space. It involves less risk because the consequence of error is less serious than is the case in an error prediction as to erroneous prediction where the substantial growth will occur.

The basis on which space for growth is uniformly provided is discussed further in dealing with the stacking formula below.

The stacking formula concept

The extent to which each of the shelves and sections is filled with books will, of course, determine the total number of shelves (and sections) required to shelve a particular collection. How many shelves and sections the individual collection will require can be determined in a number of ways. Having measured the collection in terms of linear feet, the number of linear feet of books can be divided by the number of feet to be placed on each shelf. Thus, a collection of 5,000 linear feet, assuming we are to place 2 linear feet on each shelf, would require 2,500 shelves. It may be desirable, however, to provide space for growth.

The bottom and top shelves are the most inaccessible and from the standpoint of use of the collections on a day-to-day basis, they should be allocated for expansion purposes and left vacant if at all possible.

Hence we introduce the term stacking formula which indicates several things, all relating to the section: the number of linear feet of books to be placed in the section, the fractional part of the shelf to be filled, which shelves are left empty, and the ratio of linear feet of books to the linear footage in the section (nominally 21 lin. ft.). The section is the most convenient unit for move planning, measurement, and calculation.

There are certain factors involved which relate to growth, while the other factors do not relate directly to the move per se. However, the discussion of stacking formulas necessarily brings in, at this point, certain procedural items which are actually move operations. Certain aspects of how a given stacking formula is achieved are discussed even though the main focus in this portion of the book is the nature of the stacking formula.

There are two basic methods for achieving a stacking formula:

(1) The first of these consists of setting up a basic correspondence between a set of uniform containers (booktrucks or the equivalent of booktrucks in the form of a determinant number of shelves mounted on a dolly, or wooden boxes of uniform size) and the section. The book contents of the booktruck can then be related to the section. For example, a 3-shelf booktruck with 37.5 inches interior length shelf measurement will contain 9.7 linear feet of books. This one booktruck can then be related to one specific sec-

tion and the contents of that one booktruck placed into the one section. This sets up a one-to-one correspondence between booktruck
1 and section 1, booktruck 2 and section 2, etc. It implies, and
this is quite important in the shelving operation, a multi-staged
shelving operation, that is to say, several shelving crews can work
concurrently because of the correspondence between container and
section. If one-to-one correspondence, i.e. 9.7 linear feet of books
per section is not desired, the contents of 7 booktrucks could be
shelved in 6 sections, the next 7 booktrucks into the next 6 sections.

Under this stacking formula there would be 11.3 linear feet of
books in each of the 6 sections. Similarly, 6 booktrucks can be
related to 7 sections, thus placing 8.3 linear feet of books in each
section. Under this ratio method, precise determination of the
number of linear feet of books that go in to one section is not
necessary, the main factor is that the contents of 7 booktrucks relate to 6 sections, assuming the 7:6 ratio.

Any relationships can be established, but a few such ratios are
adequate, with the 1:1 ratio being a good one for transfer of collections to the new building.

It should be remembered that this method of ratios is not necessarily limited to the use of booktrucks; containers of uniform size
can be related to the section, providing whatever density of books in
the section that may be desired.

(2) the second method also involves using booktrucks or other
containers but there is no fixed correspondence between the booktrucks (or other containers) and the sections. That is to say, the
books move from the booktrucks to the sections and designated
shelves are filled to a predetermined percentage. The booktrucks
or containers may be of varying size. The limited advantage of this
method is that it permits the use of containers of varying size in
handling the move. It does not permit concurrent unloading at several points, nor is it as exact as the ratio method.

In the second method if the stacking formula indicates 10 linear
feet in each section, on 5 shelves, then care must be exercized to

Figure 20

STACKING FORMULAS

RATIOS BETWEEN BOOKTRUCKS AND SECTIONS

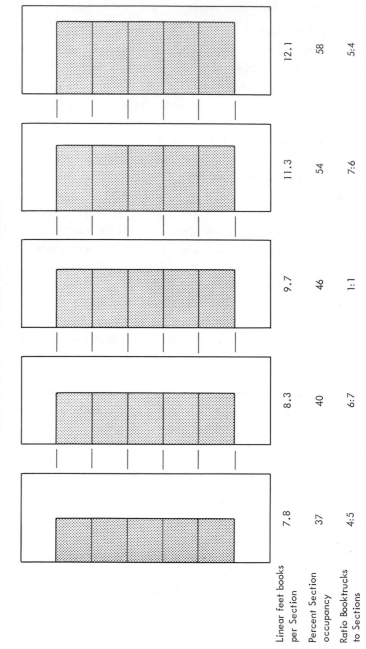

7.8	8.3	9.7	11.3	12.1
37	40	46	54	58
4:5	6:7	1:1	7:6	5:4

Linear feet books per Section

Percent Section occupancy

Ratio Booktrucks to Sections

put 2 feet or close to it on each shelf. The errors are cumulative. In the ratio method errors are not cumulative.

Stacking formulas by establishing ratio between booktrucks and sections (Method I)

The stacking formulas attainable by use of the ratio method are shown in Figure 20. The same data are exhibited in graphic form in Table 17.

Different growth provision can be made by utilization of the stack-formulas shown. In addition to the formulas shown growth requirements can be met by leaving complete sections empty on a pattern basis.

Table 17

Convenient ratios between Booktrucks
and Sections for Stacking Formulas

Number of Booktrucks[1]	Number of Sections	Linear feet of books per section	Percent of Section Occupancy[2]	Linear inches books on shelf[3]	
				5 shelves	6 shelves
4	5	7.8	37	19	16
6	7	8.3	40	20	17
1	1	9.7	46	23	19
7	6	11.3	54	27	23
5	4	12.1	58	29	24

1. Based on a booktruck with 3 interior shelves, each measuring 37.5" in length. The booktruck has an actual length of 9.375 linear feet. This is equal to 9.6875 on 9.7 linear feet of books in normal array on the shelf. Books are compressed when being moved in the booktruck and 9.7 linear feet of books in normal shelf array = 9.375 linear feet of books under compression in the booktruck. A comparable set of equivalences can be constructed where the dimension of the booktruck varies from the figures just given.

2. Based on a section of 7 shelves the shelf length is taken at 36 inches. The capacity of the section is thus 21 linear ft.

3. The number of linear inches of books on the shelves is rounded to the nearest whole inch. The columns "5 shelves" and "6 shelves" mean simply that 5 and 6 (out of the 7) are used for books, with the remainder left empty for growth purposes. Inspection of figure 20 will clarify this point.

In order to use the ratio method do all of the booktrucks have
to have exactly the same interior shelf dimension? This is desirable but if there are 25 trucks with 3 shelves of 42 inches each,
17 trucks with 3 shelves of 38 inches each, and 33 trucks with 3
shelves of 36 inches each, and the total of 75 trucks is used
throughout the move the average truck can be computed and used
in the calculations. The average is produced by:

$$\frac{(25 \text{ trucks x 3 shelves x } 42") + (17 \times 3 \times 38") + (33 \times 3 \times 36")}{75}$$

$$= \frac{8652"}{75} = 115.36", \text{ or } 9.7 \text{ linear feet.}$$

Thus, 9.7 lin. ft. would be the average truck capacity and calculations could be made in terms of this figure. The figure 9.7 linear
feet is, of course, the measurement of the booktruck's shelves.
The truck of 9.3765 inches actually contained 9.6875 linear feet of
books because of compression. This is an expansion of 3.33 percent. This expansion factor (or one which is worked out in the individual library) is likewise attributable to the booktrucks of
other sizes. The actual result in shelving will, of course, be
that some sections will receive somewhat less than others
because of variation of booktruck sizes; however, the ratio
method can be used where the variation in booktruck sizes is
small.

Stacking formulas without ratio between Booktrucks and Sections (Method 2)

The stacking formulas attainable by use of this method are shown
in Figure 21, and also in Table 18. The ones shown afford reasonable provision for growth. The growth provision can be altered by
leaving complete sections empty on a pattern basis.

Table 18 illustrates the number of shelves that can be used for
books, identifying the shelves to be used, the percentage of each
shelf to be occupied by books, and the number of linear feet of
books to be placed in the section, and also the percentage of the
section to be taken up by books (the occupancy ratio). These various
aspects of the stacking formulas will be useful in planning and vis-

Figure 21

STACKING FORMULAS, NON-RATIO BETWEEN BOOKTRUCKS AND SECTIONS

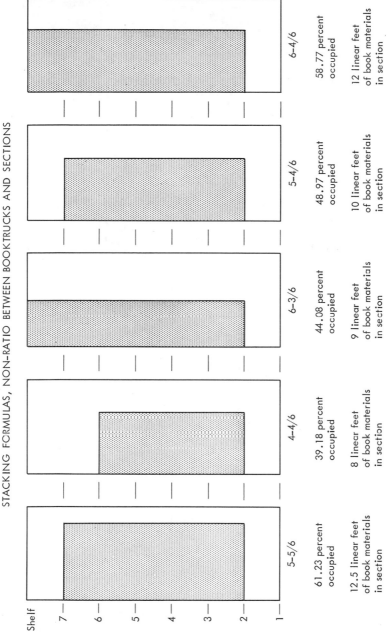

Stacking formulas, non-ratio between booktrucks and sections (Based on section consisting of 7 shelves)

Table 18

Combinations (1)	Fraction of shelf for books (2)	Linear inches of books per shelf (3)	Total linear inches of books per section (4)	Total linear feet of books per section (5)	Percent of section for books (6)	Stacking formula (7)
FOUR shelves for books Shelf 2 through 5	4/6	24	96	8	39.18	4-4/6
	5/6	30	120	10	48.97	4-5/6
FIVE shelves for books Shelf 2 through 6	3/6	18	90	7.5	36.73	5-3/6
	4/6	24	120	10	48.97	5-4/6
SIX shelves for books Shelf 2 through 7	3/6	18	108	9	44.08	6-3/6
	4/6	24	144	12	58.77	6-4/6

ualizing the placement of the collections, and will serve in the
actual moving operation to provide instructions regarding the placement of books on the shelves.

The table has been constructed principally on the assumption of
a shelf of 36 inch interior dimension to record conveniently the
density of shelving (col. 2) in multiples of one-sixth of a shelf,
even though this is not precise when translated into the linear
inch equivalent (cols. 3 and 4). The use of sixths, as a convenience in setting up the stacking formulas, becomes a practical
consideration in shelving of the books. The tolerances of shelving
books, during a move, is such that dividing up the shelf into six
increments of six inches each is a reasonable and workable interval.

Trial arrangement of the collections

Trial placements begin with two figures: the total linear feet of
material and total sections in the new building. Thus, if there are
some 60,000 linear feet of material and 6,000 sections then a stacking formula of about 10 linear feet per section is feasible. The
variations will be: (1) the different stacking formula that might be
desired to provide for greater growth in, say, Class P, and less
growth provision for Class H; (2) the necessity to make end of the
stack floors at an agreed upon sub-class (or class) and (3) the
need to compensate for errors in measurement.

Move Planning Form (Figure 22) will be of use in calculating the
relative adequacy of the tentative provisions for growth. To be kept
in mind, also, is the distinction between practical and actual capacity, previously discussed. Table 19 depicts a growth of 5 percent
annually in an average section which begins with 10 linear feet of
books; the graph displayed on Figure 23 illustrates the nature of
this growth curve.

Figure 22

Move Planning Form

Size of collection, growth rate, and stacking formula

Planning Sheet

Present size
of collection (LF)

Average annual growth rate:

Estimated size of class or collection after:

5 years:_____

10 years:_____

15 years:_____

Table 19

Growth of 10 linear feet of books at 5 percent annually over
10 year period.

Year	Linear feet of books in Section	Occupancy ratio	Volumes added annually	Total volumes in Section
0	10.00	47.6	0	100
1	10.50	50.0	5	105
2	11.03	52.5	5	110
3	11.58	55.1	6	116
4	12.15	57.8	6	122
5	12.78	60.8	6	128
6	13.41	63.8	6	134
7	14.08	67.0	7	141
8	14.78	70.3	7	148
9	15.51	73.8	7	155
10	16.28	77.5	8	163

The trial placement continues by considering a provisional breaking point at the end of a stack floor. If Class AC through Class BX comprises 9,685 linear feet of books and the first stack floor has a total of 960 sections, this means that slightly more than 10 linear feet per section will be required. We might consider placing Class CA or CB on our first stack floor, but this decision has to be taken in the context of the subject classes remaining. Placing additional classes on the first floor might mean overcrowding the first floor and leaving the second floor lightly shelved. The trial placement must deal with all of the subject classes and all of the stack floors since what is done on any one floor will affect the other floors. Different stacking formulas to meet different growth requirements must be considered. The selection of breaking points at the end of stack floors, thus, usually results in some compressing or loosening in order to fit the end of a class or sub-class to the end of a stack floor. At

Figure 23

GRAPH OF ACTUAL AND PRACTICAL CAPACITY OF A SECTION

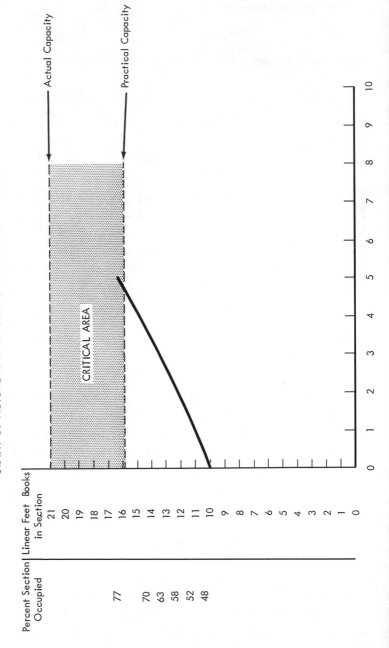

any rate, we may feel that ending the first floor with BX provides good balance with respect to the remaining classes and the remaining stack levels.

The most desirable stacking formula from the standpoint of the mechanics of moving, and a desirable one as well from the standpoint of providing liberal growth, is one booktruck per section under the ratio method. The single-loaded booktruck holds 9.7 linear feet of books. If 9.7 linear feet of books are placed in each section, 9,685 linear feet of books will require 998 sections; however, only 960 sections are available. How can this be handled under the ratio method?

The ratio of 1 booktruck to 1 section can be used for part of the first stack floor and another ratio elsewhere on this floor. This other ratio will have to put more than 9.7 linear feet in each section. Table 17 indicates that the ratio of 7 booktrucks to 6 sections results in 11.3 linear feet per section.

The number of sections to be filled at each ratio can be calculated as follows:

Let x = the number of sections to be filled at a certain amount, and 9.7 x = number of Sections to be filled at 9.7 linear feet each 11.3 (960 — x) = number of sections to be filled at 11.3 linear feet each

$$9.7 x + 11.3 (960 - x) = 9465 \text{ linear feet}$$
$$9.7 x + 10,848 - 11.3 x = 9465$$
$$1.6 x = 1383$$
$$x = 864 \text{ sections}$$

Thus 864 sections can be filled at 9.7 linear feet each, that is, 1 booktruck: 1 section, and

$$960 - 864 = 96 \text{ sections},$$

can be filled at 11.3 linear feet each, that is, 7 booktrucks : 6 sections.

Check:

864 sections x 9.7 linear feet each = 8381 linear feet

96 sections x 11.3 linear feet each = <u>1084</u> linear feet

Total 9465 linear feet.

At what point we use the 1:1 ratio and where we use the 7:6
ratio depends upon the individual circumstances; a good general
plan is to use one ratio then another in fairly long runs; for example, the 1:1 ratio might be used for 400 sections, then the 7:6
ratio for 48 sections, then 464 on the 1:1 ratio, followed by the
48 at the 7:6 ratio.

To continue this example, let us assume that we have the 9,465
linear feet of books and 960 sections but that we wish to leave
every 10th section vacant; this would mean a total of 48 sections
left empty ($\frac{960}{20}$ = 48). This means that 912 sections would be
available for 9,465 linear feet of books. To determine how many
sections can be filled at the 1:1 ratio and how many at the 7:6 ratio
the equation is as follows:

9.7 x + 11.3 (912 — x) = 9,465

9.7 x + 10,306 — 11.3 x = 9465

$$1.6 \ x \qquad = \qquad 841$$

$$x \qquad = \qquad 526 \text{ sections to be filled at}$$

9.7 linear feet each and 912 — 526 — 326 sections to be
filled at 11.3 linear feet each.

Check:

526 sections x 9.7 linear feet each = 5,102

386 sections x 11.3 linear feet each = 4,362

Total   9,464

These are the steps and trials which will help achieve a bal-
anced arrangement in the new building. The compensations which
are made, in the course of the move to take care of an over-es-
timate or under-estimate are taken up in Chapter V. Basically,
however, such compensations are made by raising or lowering the
density of the stacking formula (from 1:1 to 7:6 or from 1:1 to 4:5)
as we pass certain check points in the course of the moving.

The same mechanics would be used with stacking formulas not
based on correspondence between booktrucks and sections. Using
the same figures as in the previous example, that is, 9,465 lin.
ft. of books, 960 sections, assuming again that we wish every 20
section entirely empty, thus leaving 912 sections.

$\frac{9,465}{912}$ = 10.3 approx. linear feet as the average content per
section Figure 21 shows that the closest stacking formula "5 - 4/6"
i.e., 5 shelves out of the 7 used, each of the 5 filled 4/6 with
books, would place 10 linear feet in each section. Thus, $\frac{9,465}{10}$ =
947 sections. We have only 912 sections. Thus, we will want a
stacking formula to be used in conjunction with the one mentioned,
that is, we will want to use 10 lin. ft. per section for some of the
sections, and something higher for the remainder of the 896 sections. A convenient formula places 12.5 linear feet in the section.

Returning to the formula to ascertain how many sections need
to be filled at 10 linear feet and how many need to be filled at 12.5
linear feet

$$10x + 12.5 (912 - x) = 9465 \text{ lin. ft.}$$
$$10x + 11,400 - 12.5x = 9465$$
$$2.5 x = 1935$$
$$x = 774 \text{ sections}$$

can be filled at 10 lin. ft. each; and 912 -- 774 or 138
sections can be filled at 12.5 lin. ft.

Check:

774 sections x 10 lin. ft. each = 7740
138 sections x 12.5 lin. ft. each =1725
                    Total   9465

The location of books and the location of service points

The relative value of bookstack areas declines roughly in proportion to the increasing distance from the booklift on any particular level. The prime stack location would be defined by a certain
radius extending from the vertical axis at the stack elevator opening.
Several radii can be indicated on the stack plans by drawing a number of concentric circles with the bookstack elevator entrance as a
center, utilizing radii of 50, 75, and 100 feet. This will serve as
an indication of the proportions existing in the new building and
provides an idea of the relative spaciousness of those areas pos-
sessing relatively greater "value".

The concept of variation in value of given areas in relation to
distance from the booklift servicing the circulation desk in the read-

ing room has pragmatic implications: if a collection used relatively frequently is placed near the booklift this provides an important advantage in avoiding thousands of excess steps in obtaining and replacing volumes. The number of steps taken by the library assistant in the circulation department to procure a single book and the converse operation, shelving it, is an operation which will be performed thousands of times during the life of the building, or even in the life of a particular collection in a specific area or areas.

Accordingly, the areas nearest the booklift (on all levels) represent space of greater value than do more remote areas. This, in turn, suggests that the most used materials should be situated in the locations of greater value.

This factor of relative value of bookstack areas must be considered in the context of the type of library involved (and the configuration of the building). A library not committed to a single classification for all its library materials is in better position to place relatively greater used materials in the prime stack areas. In a library in which the entire collection is in classification order (and in open stack) the concept of area value is greatly diminished.

Should all of the areas be regarded as immediately usable? Provided the new building and its bookstack capacity is relatively large in comparison to the size of the book collections, thought may be given to leaving certain areas vacant. These areas left vacant might be those of least value. The purpose of introducing this alternative -- again assuming that the total shelf capacity in the new building is substantially larger than the book collection -- is the alternative of centralizing or decentralizing the collections (either leaving relatively little or relatively much space for growth on the shelves), the latter at the expense of diminished accessibility by the circulation department. Particularly if the building is one in which the levels are very large consideration should be given to leaving the further reaches entirely vacant, using the areas within a reasonable distance from the booklift.

This will reduce the number of steps in securing the replacing volumes for a reasonably long time.

The trial placement of the collections should be entered on a set of stack floor plans. When the final version of the arrangement of the collection has been determined a directory of the collection can be reproduced well before for the opening of the building for service. The plotting of the arrangement on the stack plan should be in terms of the total assigned to each of the individual floors,

At this stage another set of documents becomes very important. A spare set of stack plans should be cut up in terms of areas and reproduced at a substantial enlargement (Figure 25).

The enlargements should then be mounted on stiff cardboard and labelled to indicate: the floor and area number; the direction of shelving indicated by an arrow, with indication of beginning section; and the number of sections in the area; the number to be left empty for growth purposes (if known at this time); and the net total for shelving. They should be put in consecutive order, in the sequence to be followed in shelving.

Shelving sets or long runs

In shelving sets or "long runs" in the new areas the question may arise, "Why not shelve the long runs continuously, filling each shelf to capacity, since no growth will occur within the long runs?" The long runs may, in fact, be shelved continuously but a number of adjustments are required. It is important to state, however, the advantage of not shelving long runs continuously: Treating all the volumes of a given collection according to a single stacking formula, without deviation, provides an automatic procedure for shelving at move time -- no special procedures are necessary -- and periodic pockets of space are built into the entire collection. These pockets of space, even though present within long runs, can be utilized in the future by virtue of only minor shifting.

Bookends or book supports

A check should be made of the number of books ends required for the new building bookstack areas. Figures should be on hand as to the number of bookends available from the present building, assuming that the type used is satisfactory. The relevant data on new

Figure 24

DIAGRAM OF AN AREA IN UCLA LIBRARY BUILDING

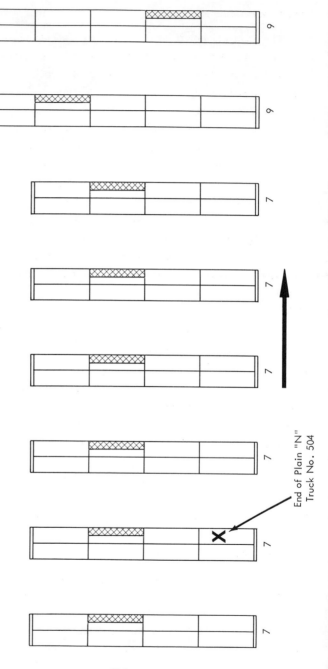

End of Plain "N"
Truck No. 504

building bookend needs can readily be derived from the stacking
formula to be used; this will indicate whether, for example, the
top and bottom shelf will be empty. The number of sections multiplied by the number of non-empty shelves per section will produce the number of shelves requiring bookends. This will constitute
the direct and immediate need. The number on hand from the present building taken from this total will give the net amount of bookends needed. The question of "reserve" bookends should be considered, that is, bookends for the empty shelves.

The kind or type of bookend should be given careful attention.
For larger volumes the so-called folio bookend is warranted; for
smaller volumes the smaller bookend with a flange to prevent
"knifing" of books is adequate. Both the large and the small bookends should be equipped with cork or plastic pads to avoid scratch-
ing of the metal book shelf.

Chapter V

The Moving Operation: From Present to New Building

Purpose

The present chapter is divided into two parts. The first considers the general planning for moving from the present to the new building. This covers the spectrum from manpower to be utilized, through the presentation of principles to make the changeover from present to new building with least interruption of basic library services and routines. The second portion is devoted to methodology, techniques, and procedures. The second portion discusses, for example, the procedures relating to booktrucks, the labor and supervision involved in moving, and charting the techniques.

The manpower situation

Who will do the actual moving? The moving can be accomplished by the regular library staff or by non-library personnel. Non-library personnel may be either professional movers or personnel from the university's buildings and grounds department, or other local labor. The use of Library staff for a large-scale, protracted move is seriously to be questioned. The extent to which library personnel are invested in the moving operation represents the extent to which regular library operations suffer. The physical job of packing books or loading them from shelf onto booktruck and placing them on the shelves in the new building is a physically arduous task. Attention must be given to the possibility of physical disability or accidents and loss of time which might occur. These are reasons for not utilizing regular library staff members. The advantage, on the other hand, of using regular library staff members is that they know the book collections, are used to handling books, and can be depended upon to treat books carefully.

The choice (if there is one) between professional movers and the buildings and grounds department would have to be made on the

basis of the special factors in each situation. In general, moving
concerns are experienced in performing the physically exacting task
of moving a library, with respect to both furniture and equipment,
and books. The professional moving concern, is usually a
versatile organization, experienced in moving procedures,
and can provide a continuous supply of trained manpower
and equipment to accomplish the job on schedule.

The deadline or target date set for completion, since it would
normally be arranged with the professional mover on a contract
basis, becomes a firm date. This, of course, is a most important
consideration in the planning of library services and the other con-
tingencies faced by the library during such a critical occasion as
moving time.

A buildings and grounds department which has had moving experience would also rank high. The performance of the UCLA's Department of Buildings and Grounds, in the UCLA move, was excellent.

A number of items require consideration if there is a choice
between a professional mover and the local facility available (buildings and grounds department). One is the continuity of the labor
supply. Whether the move is small, medium, or large, adequate
assurance ought to exist that sufficient manpower will be available
on a day-to-day basis to ensure completion of the move on schedule.

The experience of the staff should be examined. To what extent
is the labor force seasoned in moving, not necessarily in the sense
of handling book materials, but in the sense of moving per se? This
is a question of physical ability, as well as the matter of expertise
in the art and science of moving. The relative degree of experience
exerts an influence, of course, on the daily production. The matter
of equipment should also be looked into: will the non-library personnel provide the necessary equipment and how adequate is it? The
care which books and furniture and equipment will receive represents another factor that should be checked. The move director
will have to make a judgment as to the probable reliability of the

labor source being considered. Perhaps, here, the record of previous work can be evaluated as an aid in decision making.

In summary, we have set down some of the general considerations which merit attention in making a choice with respect to the source of moving manpower. The library administrator, or move director, then has to examine the local resources available to him (professional movers, manpower from within the University community, etc.) on the basis of these considerations and make his best estimate and decision.

Role of library staff members

We may think of the move in the sense of division of labor. We have, on one hand, the supervisory or directing aspects; on the other hand, we have the physical labor involved. As pointed out it is not desirable for library staff members to move the library in the physical sense, but consideration should be given to having library staff members performing the guiding and directing operations during the actual moving. They should supervise the withdrawal of books from the shelves to ensure that they are taken in proper sequence and the placement of books on the shelves in the new building. The library staff is better equipped to supervise the moving of library materials than is the mover. Every move requires a substantial investment of library staff time. In both the NLM and UCLA moves the staff was fully taxed by regular work and by the planning and supervision of the move duties.

An early finding of the nature and extent of the necessary manpower investment should obviously be made, since outside assistance, be it professional movers or local labor supply, may involve considerable advance scheduling, negotiation, and funding. The nature of this manpower investment relates to the functions and operations such assistance will provide. If a professional mover is to be assigned the job, the moving concern will study the move, estimate the number of men, time, and equipment, required. If outside help other than professional movers is assigned the job, then it is well for the library staff to calculate the requirements of the move in somewhat more precise terms to assure that the requisite manpower will be available on a continuing, day-to-day basis.

The estimate, of course, depends on the size of the collection, techniques, manpower, etc. The present chapter should be examined in its entirety prior to making the estimates.

There should be continuous readiness once the move is begun and the moving should proceed uninterruptedly throughout the entire cycle. The professional mover will customarily be prepared to do this. If outside help other than professional movers are involved, the estimates of manpower and equipment will have to be studied carefully to assure uninterrupted moving. This is an economic factor: the moving, once begun, must continue since it is wasteful to have a labor force committed for a number of days, then have the move readiness on the part of the library collapse, leaving the labor force with nothing to do.

The scheduling of the move on the part of the library's move director must ensure that the moving readiness of the library unfolds on schedule so that first this part of the library is ready, then that part, etc. These parts may be combinations of furniture and equipment and book collections, but the main consideration is that there must be material on hand and in condition to move at the appropriate time.

Move Committee Activity

Six months before "M Day" (beginning of the move) the master move plan should be refined. The six month period mentioned is subject to adjustment dependent upon the complexity of the given move; it is well, however, to err on the side of beginning this refinement early. At this stage, detailed procedures must be developed and tested, specific tasks assigned covering final preparations, and the order, grouping, and scheduling established by which the functional elements of the library are moved. The Committee should include a representative from each major administrative unit of the library. Later, it may prove desirable to increase this number, dependent upon the size and complexity of the organizational unit concerned. Except for the smallest units, at least two representatives are indicated so that on moving day there will be adequate

direction and supervision available at both ends of the move for
each element being moved.

Costs

How much will it cost? There are a number of reasons why
costs can not be estimated here. The size and complexity of the
move will vary from library to library. Costs are different in different geographic areas. Much depends, too, upon the proportion
of the move done by regular library staff. If professional movers
do the job the cost will usually be determined by bidding. Seasonal
variations in the moving industry and the extent of competition will
affect the price. Because of all of these variables no meaningful
treatment of costs can be offered here.

Describing and defining the job for the move organization

Whether a professional mover or other non-library labor force
is to perform the physical job of moving, it is essential to set a-
side a period of time to acquaint the move organization with the
total job. This briefing should cover actual inspection of the present
and new building, and entrances, exists, elevators, and loading
platforms in both buildings. The move plan should be presented by
the Library's move director, reviewing the various aspects and requirements of the plan.

The sequence of events, if an invitation to bid is decided upon,
is:

1. preparing and issuing the invitation which
   specifies when the premises (present and
   new buildings) may be inspected.

2. inspection of the present and new building
   by prospective bidder. Question and answer
   period -- usually conducted under the supervision and administration of the administrative office responsible for issuance of invitation to bid and award of contract. (The question and answer period is normally limited to
   questions of fact, with respect to the language
   in the invitation and the question, and the answer is repeated for all at the briefing ses-
   sion).

The invitation to bid, in setting forth the expectations and requirements of the Library, is of value whether the entire bid procedure is adopted or not. Its merit consists, basically, in its
characterization of who does what and this is precisely the type of
statement or understanding which is required between the library
and the manpower force in the move operation. The respective roles
of the library staff members and those of the mover should be defined; this is not only essential for a contract, but it is equally important in the practical sense of the moving. There should be a
clear and precise statement of what is required of the mover, what
he is to do (and what he is not to do). Excerpts from the National
Library of Medicine contract and excerpts from the data prepared
for the UCLA Library move are given in the appendix.

The probable duration of the move

The duration of the move will have to be an estimate and this
estimate is the result of an equation into which we have put a great
many terms: amount of manpower, its efficiency, magnitude of the
book collection, accessibility of the book collection, nature and extent of equipment available, etc. However, once these and other
factors have been reviewed with a given library move in mind an
estimate can be formed and a probable duration of the move ar-
rived at. There are a number of reasons why this should be worked
out. First, preliminary discussions with the moving organization
will be more realistically pursued after review of the given library
situation in the context of the data presented here. The estimated
duration is an important piece of information in relation to the state
of construction of the new building, that is, the date on which the
new building is in a state of readiness to receive books and furniture.

The probable date the new building is ready to receive books
and furniture is an important estimate. This doesn't mean that the
new building is completed. It will generally, however, be desirable
to plan on beginning the move on the date fixed for the new building's readiness to receive books or on a date shortly thereafter.
In the move planning the date on which the new building will be

ready to receive books will not normally be firm. As stated, it is usually desirable to plan to begin the move for the date (or shortly thereafter) that the new building is ready to receive books. All this is of course based on the premise that the new building is to be occupied as soon as possible.

The move of the book collections, moreover, will probably continue after the new building has become the center of operations. In both the NLM and UCLA moves from 60 to 65 percent of the collections had been moved at the time the new building became the center of operations.

There are a number of important dates, then, which ought to be estimated some months ahead of the planned move -- and these estimates have to be periodically examined and "firmed up" as time goes on. These key dates are:

(1) date on which to begin the move;

(2) probable date on which the move will end;

(3) probable date that the new building is in state of readiness for move to begin;

(4) date on which the new building is to be the center of operations.

An aid in making estimates as to the duration of a move is the simulated move.

Once a number of factors have been set down, certain agreed-upon work procedures adopted, it is very desirable to devote a day to an actual test exercise to gauge time requirements and also to create an awareness of actual conditions to be faced. The test exercise is recommended since it is an excellent proving ground to check procedures, their advantages and shortcomings. The simulated move will also provide an indication of the satisfactory nature of the move route, the loading platforms, etc., and other detailed aspects of the move operation which -- given individual library situations -- can only come to light by actual test. The relative size and complexity of the total job will affect the duration of the move. The nature of the book materials (e.g., the extent of rare book materials, photographs, maps, and other special forms of material) and the quantities of furniture and equipment will play an important part in gaug-

Figure 25

PHASES OF THE MOVE.

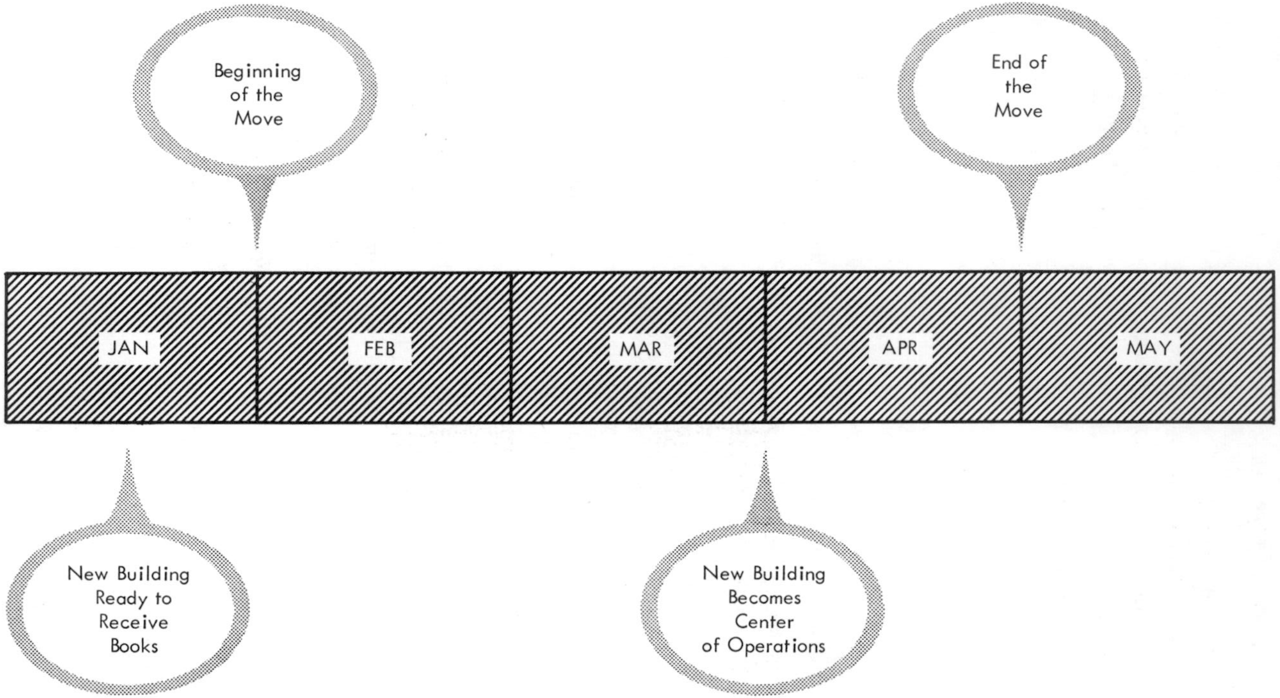

End of the Move

Beginning of the Move

New Building Becomes Center of Operations

New Building Ready to Receive Books

JAN   FEB   MAR   APR   MAY

ing the duration. The size of the manpower force and the extent of
the material (equipment such as boxes, booktrucks, moving vans,
if used, etc.) also relate importantly to the number of days the
move will require. Increased tempo requires a larger and larger
input to realize a proportionate rate of increase in production. The
law of diminshing returns applies and increased manpower and moving equipment brings collateral needs which will also have to be
augmented in certain proportions; these include supervisory personnel, increases in the number of entrances and exits, loading
platforms, etc.

The actual dates involved in the NLM and UCLA Library moves
are shown in Table 19a.

Table 19a.

NLM and UCLA Library move schedules

	Move beginning	Center of operations	Conclusion
NLM	March 5 (1962)	April 16	May 3
UCLA	June 29 (1964)	August 3	August 20

The order of the move and the changeover

The order of the move ought to be such that there is minimum
interruption of library services. Proper management of the move,
especially in the scheduling or timing, can achieve this goal.

To describe the order of the move we wish to make use of the
concept center of operations. We can picture the present building
as the center of operations, the place from which service is made
available to the clientele in the form of providing the card catalog,
reference and circulation service, interlibrary loan service.

At some point in time the new building will supplement the new
building in performing this set of functions. This transition of the
center of operations from the present building to the new building is

termed the changeover. The changeover is critical and represents
the goal of the entire move planning, because it is at this time that
the new building, at one stroke, becomes fully operational and
serves as the new center of operations. (If the new building represents a second or auxiliary building, then the changeover is critical
with respect to the functions which the new building is intended to
meet).

Some time before changeover, the move will be initiated.

During Phase 1 of the move the library materials of infrequent
use ought to be moved first. The build-up, ideally, should advance
to more frequently used materials. Materials which have been
moved to the new building and which are required for reader service in the present building can be retrieved and serviced from the
present building, since it is the center of operations at this time.

At some time close to changeover, Phase 2 of the move can
be initiated. This will cover the moving of the most essential book
materials and supporting materials, including the reference room
collection, the card catalog, the serial record, the photoduplication
equipment, etc. It is desirable that Phase 2 be done over a weekend or a time when library service demands are low.

Phase 3 represents the changeover itself and the assumption by
the new building of its role as center of operations. The staff will
report to the new building and perform its regular functions there.
Service to readers will be provided from the new building. Many
volumes of book material may still remain in the present building
but these will now be serviced from the new center of operations.

The move begins with the books and is followed at some later
time by the move of departments with their furniture and equipment.
There would be concurrent moving of books and equipment (such as
office machines, files etc.) In general the public service department,
along with the public card catalog, would be moved at the last possible time. An earlier move is indicated, then, for the public service
functions, except that the move of the catalog Department (with the
catalog shelflist) would have to be timed close to the public
functions move.

In the NLM move, the target date selected for the new building
to be the center of operations was April 16, 1962. This was designated some weeks in advance after careful estimates and check of
schedules. The move began on March 5, marking the beginning of
Phase 1. Phase 1 continued until April 11. During Phase 1 the
lesser used library materials were moved to the new building. The
very few materials required for reader and interlibrary loan service were returned to the present building on the empty moving vans
returning to Washington from the new building in Bethesda; these
book materials were serviced from the present building which was
the center of operations at that time.

Phase 2 began on April 12. During this period the most essential book materials and supporting equipment, including the
reference collection in the reading room, the card catalog, the
serial record, the photoduplication equipment were moved to the
new building. Phase 2 ended on April 14 (Saturday).

Phase 3 opened with the changeover -- the opening of the new
building on Monday, April 16, the new building then supplanting the
old building on this date as the center of operations. Staff reported
to the new building on April 16, service to readers (reference and
circulation) and interlibrary loan service proceeded from the new
building. At this time some 63 percent of the book collections had
been moved. The more essential book collections were in place in
the new building and some 17,000 linear feet of material, which
remained in the old building, was retrieved upon call from the new
building. The 17,000 linear feet of material was completely moved
into the new building by May 3, 1962, marking the end of Phase 3
and of the move.

The description of the process applied to the UCLA move is as
follows. The target date selected for the new building to be the center of operations was August 3, 1964. The move began on June 29
1964 and this marked the beginning of Phase One. It should be noted
that unlike the NLM move which began with lesser-used materials,
the UCLA move began with the beginning of the LC classification.
Books required for circulation service in the present building were

Table 19 b.

Comparison of National Library of Medicine and UCLA Library Master Move Plans

National Library of Medicine move		UCLA Library move	
Period	Order of the Departmental Moves	Period	Order of the Departmental Moves
March 5 1962 [Monday] TO April 6 [Friday] Workdays: 25	April 5: Bibliographic Services Division.	June 29 [Monday] (1964) TO July 24 [Friday] Workdays: 20	July 23 24 Acquisitions Dept.
April 9 [Monday] TO April 14 [Saturday] Library closed: Apr. 13, 14. Workdays: 6	April 10: Technical Services Div. 11: " " " 12: " " " (incl. shelflist) 13: Reference Services Div. and Public Card Catalog 14: Reference, Services Div, Reading Rm/collection, & Public Card Catalog.	July 27 [Monday] TO August 1 [Saturday] Library closed: July 31 & Aug.1 Workdays: 6	July 27: Serials Dept. 28: Serials Dept. 29: Catalog Dept. 30: Catalog Dept., Shelflist, Read. Rm. coll. 31: Public Card Catalog, Ref. Dept., Read Rm. coll. Aug. 1: Public Card Catalog, Ref. Dept., Read Rm. coll.
April 16	CHANGEOVER	August 3	CHANGEOVER

Table 19 b. (cont.)

Comparison of National Library of Medicine and UCLA Library Master Move Plans

National Library of Medicine move		UCLA Library move	
Period	Order of the Departmental Move	Period	Order of the Departmental Move
[Monday] TO May 3 [Thursday] Workdays: 14	April 16: Office of the Director April 17: Binding Section	[Monday] TO August 20 [Thursday] Workdays: 14	Aug. 3: Circulation Dept. (completion) 4: Office of the Librarian

TOTAL CALENDAR DAYS: 60 TOTAL WORKDAYS: 45   TOTAL CALENDAR DAYS: 53 TOTAL WORKDAYS: 40

transmitted via pneumatic tube.

Phase Two began on July 27, (Monday). At this time Classes
A through J were moved to the new building. Phase Two ended on
August 1 (Saturday).

Phase Three opened with the changeover, and the opening of
the new building on August 3, the new building then supplanting the
present as the center of library operations. At this time some 65
percent of the book collections had been moved, Classes A through
PE. Some 17,000 linear feet remained in the present building. This
material was moved into the new building by August 20 marking the
end of Phase Three and the end of the move. The organization of
the NLM and UCLA moves into phases and the order of the moves
are shown in Table 19b.

Obviously the more material which can be moved in Phase 1
the better. However, the designation of the new building as center
of operations is the target. If we have too much material moved
during Phase 1 too much material must be brought back from the
new building for service in the present building.

On the other hand, if Phase 1 covers too little material, then
the retrieval of book materials from the old building for servicing
in the new building may be substantial. The important thing about
the changeover is that a balance should be sought. Phase One should
handle a large group of materials; if possible, these should be gen-
erate relatively little reader or service use. Phase Two should be
as short as possible, sufficient to move the essential materials
and supporting equipment. Phase Three to a large extent, describes
the consequences of the actions taken in Phase One and Two.

In Phase One we are beginning to move. It is far better to
have Phase One as a sort of proving ground, to gain experience in
moving and to perfect techniques. Errors can be rectified more
easily at this stage.

The following is a hypothetical sequence of events. It is assumed that in January word is received from the contractor that
the building will be completed in April; further checking leads to
decision by the move director that the changeover ought to be April

5 and that moving ought to be initiated on March 15.

The diagram sketches the timing (Figure 26).

Opening of new building stack areas to clientele

When we state the new building becomes the center of operations at changeover time we have indicated that services (reference and circulation, etc.) will be provided to the clientele at the new building. In our previous discussion we remarked that a certain proportion of the book materials might still be in the "old" building. At the National Library of Medicine, for example, 37 percent of the book material was still in the old building at the changeover time. This was suitable for a closed stack library such as NLM. An open stack library, while extending service in the new building on changeover date has a serious problem of book stock.

When should readers be permitted to enter the bookstack areas? Should this occur concurrently with changeover? Two reasonable solutions would be: (1) Open up at changeover such floors (or levels) as have been completely shelved at the time; or (2) defer all access to the bookstack areas from changeover through completion of the move, that is, until all of the collection has been shelved. In the UCLA move the first alternative was chosen; at changeover Floors 2,3 and about 90 percent of Floor 4 were shelved at changeover. Access was granted to Floors 2, and 3 and in a few days to Floor 4. Access to Floor 5 was made in installments by cordoning off areas by ropes.

Methods of moving books from the present to the new building

A number of methods may be used to transfer book materials from one building to another. Distance and value of the books may be factors. For example, the move of the History of Medicine Division of the National Library of Medicine from Cleveland, Ohio, to Bethesda, Maryland used water-proof cartons hauled by moving vans. The move of the main NLM collections from the old building in Washington, D.C. to the new building in Bethesda, Maryland, a distance of 11 miles, used booktrucks and bookcarts hauled by moving vans. The UCLA Library move, involving a like amount of

Figure 26

Diagram of move Operations

MARCH 1-14	MARCH 15	MARCH 16-31	APRIL 1-4	APRIL 5	APRIL 6
	Beginning of MOVE DAY	Moving	Move of Critical Materials	CHANGE-OVER	Moving
		PHASE ONE	PHASE TWO	PHASE THREE	
PRESENT BUILDING AS THE CENTER OF OPERATIONS			NEW BUILDING AS THE CENTER OF OPERATIONS		

book material was made use of a fleet of some 120 booktrucks and small flatbed trucks holding 15 booktrucks each. The distance involved in the UCLA move was about one-half mile.

Cardboard cartons have been used, are inexpensive, but pose certain problems. Book boxes, an open box about 36 inches in length with handles, offer another expedient. These can be fabricated so that they may be stacked easily.

The use of a conveyer belt offers another possibility. This achieves rapidity of movement, within certain limits, is limited to a relatively short distances. Other conveyance is required to get books to and from the conveyer belt.

The booktruck offers the important advantage of mobility. It is, in effect, a box on wheels which can carry books from the shelves in the given section to the section in the new building, old shelf to new shelf, without intermediate rehandling. Getting boxes or cardboard cartons in and out of moving vans means lifting them; if the move doesn't involve the moving van, then the boxes or card-= board cartons would require some other conveyance. The booktruck is its own conveyance and is compatible with long moves (placement on moving van) as well as for short distance moves (building to building or within building moves).

The disadvantage of using a booktruck, however, is that large numbers are required and the demand for booktrucks will far outweigh the available supply. The principle of the booktruck can be utilized with a substitute contrived to reduce the need for booktrucks. Either the bookcart, simply 3 shelves with interior length of 36 inches, or some other box arrangements on a dolly satisfies the principle and the requirement. The bookcart is an inexpensive alternative which provides the same advantages of a booktruck. Basically it is a box fabricated from rough lumber with interior length of 36 inches, 15 inches in height, and 15 inches in depth. The sides are so prepared that a simple locking device will hold the three boxes together without nails (cf. Figure 2). When mounted on a dolly we have the equivalent of a booktruck. Following the move the bookcarts can be taken apart and put to a number of useful purposes, e.g., exchange shipments, storage, etc.

Variations of this arrangement which may be more practicable can be devised to suit the individual library requirement.

The use of booktrucks or bookcarts of uniform size will make possible the use of the correspondence between booktruck and section previously described.

Manpower requirements

The number of workers committed to the move can be outlined in some detail. There will, of course, be variations depending upon the design of the building and location of exits, etc. This outline is based on the use of booktrucks.

The manpower needs in the present building consist of one library staff member in the bookstack areas. His responsibility is to guide the removal of books from the shelf to assure that they are drawn in the proper order and that they are arranged on the booktruck in correct order. From four to six non-library workers would be employed. The range of four to six persons depends on the configuration of the building.

The first worker would pull the books from the shelf, hand them to the second worker for placement on the booktruck. At the ends of aisles the first worker could place the books on the truck by himself; however, as the move advances into the aisle the two man team arrangement is superior. A third worker is needed to push the loaded booktruck to the elevator; this worker also returns empty booktrucks as the move progresses. This third worker could operate the elevator and push the booktrucks to the loading platform. In most instances, however, a fourth worker who runs the elevator and pushes the booktrucks from the exit to the loading platform is desirable. A fifth worker will be required at the loading platform to roll the booktrucks onto the moving van or truck. A sixth person to assist in the vacuum cleaning would be desirable. The six workers should be regarded as a team with rotation of duties highly desirable since the physical demands of the operations of the first two workers are greater than those of the others.

There are other duties. When empty vans are returned from the

new building to the present building, they have to be distributed
to the proper area. The fourth, fifth and sixth workers would perform this job.

Supervision of the non-Library crew would require a seventh
person. Accordingly, we have a "team" made up of the supervisor,
and six workers; possibly five, but certainly no less than four.

As indicated, there would be one library staff member guiding
the movers in pulling the volumes from the shelves in the stack
area. There would also be a library staff member in charge of the
present building moving operations; this staff member would patrol
the stack area, loading platform and be available for decision.

The library staff in the bookstack area where the loading occurs
would of course be augmented if there were materials to be blended
in. The manpower requirements for the mover are set forth in
Table 20.

Table 20
Probable manpower requirements for the mover (present
building

Number of workers	Function	Work Station
1	Pull books from shelves	Bookstack area
1	Place books on book-truck	Bookstack area
1	Push booktruck to elevator	Bookstack area and elevator
1	Operate elevator	Elevator
1	Push booktruck from elevator to loading platform	Ground level and elevator exit
1	Push booktruck onto moving van and operate vacuum cleaner	Loading platform area
1	Supervisor, moving organization	Library (stack area and loading platform

The manpower needed by the mover in the new building is essentially the same as for the present building, except the work
force can be augmented to permit concurrent shelving if the correspondence between booktrucks and sections has been set up. The

manpower requirements for the mover are set forth in Table 21.

Table 21

Probable manpower requirements for the
mover (new building)

Number of workers	Function	Work Station
1	Supervisor, moving organization	Library stack area and loading platform
1	Push booktrucks from moving van to loading platform and to elevator	Loading platform area
1	Operate elevator	Elevator
1	Push booktrucks from elevator exit to stack area	Bookstack and elevator areas
1	Transfer books from booktrucks to intermediate booktrucks	Bookstack area
2	Shelve Books	Bookstack area

Operations in the present building stacks

Booktrucks are single loaded with books, spines up, on all three
shelves. A booktruck with 37.5 inches interior length, three shelves,
totals 9.375 linear feet and will hold 9.7 linear feet of books in
normal shelf array on the average, the difference being accounted
for by compression when the books are inserted tightly in the truck.
(If booktrucks of a different interior length are used the comparable
figures will have to be developed).

In terms of weight the single-loaded truck will average about
300 lbs. including the weight of the truck itself, which is about 75
lbs. Aside from the fact that the move is calculated around the
single-loaded booktruck, there are important advantages to single-
loading rather than double loading. The latter would be a slow process in the stack aisles and the manipulation of the added weight
would be delaying. Increased likelihood of damage to books is present also.

The books should be compressed so that they will not fall off the truck. Where necessary a wooden "dummy" should be inserted between last book and edge of truck. The dummies should be of 3/4 inch width.

The placards should be prepared well before move time. These should be of cardboard, approximately 10" x 14" in size, so as to stand out well above the top of the booktruck. The placards should be numbered with fluid marking pencil in large numerals on both sides of placard. The number sequence should be in sets of from 1 to 1,000 and the different sets should be numbered in different colors. It is good practice to begin the new floor in the new building with a new set; this assists in gauging the progress of shelving. The number of the last book truck for a given floor will be known and word can be conveyed to the staff in the present building to begin with a new set of placards. The placards should not be re-used.

The reason for preparing pre-numbered signs or placards for insertion in the loaded booktruck, rather than marking or attaching a "permanent" number to each booktruck is simply that in this way we avoid the arrangement of booktrucks themselves; equally important, the running total of booktruck numbers gives us a statistical check on our measurement since we know average booktruck capacity.

The booktrucks to be used for the move should be marshalled in the stack areas of the present building for the move operation. The library staff member in charge should insert the placard bearing the truck number after the truck has been fully loaded. He is, in effect, certifying the correctness of the order.

Moving books located outside present building's main bookstacks

The measurement of books located outside the present stacks and the various ways of merging such books were discussed in earlier chapters. These should be reviewed as background for handling mergers as part of the move. The five methods of merging are:

(1) Shelving the minor group with the major group in advance of the move;

(2) Blending the minor group into the major group
during the move;

(3) Designating specific sections to be empty in the
new building to receive the minor group at a
later date, the minor group usually being located,
in a separate building and in concentrated form
(e.g., long run or set);

(4) Designating sections to be empty on the basis of
a pattern (e.g. every 5th section empty) to receive the minor group at a later date, the minor
group usually being located in a separate building and spread out over a class or sub-class.

(5) Shelving the minor group after the move.

The different methods are now discussed from the standpoint of
actual move procedures.

Method 1: This requires no elaboration. It is a pre-move activity
and is recommended when the shelf space for the major group permits the intershelving.

Method 2: This concerns the merging of books which can conveniently be brought into the main bookstack areas of the present
building for blending into the main collection. This usually involves
a group of books under a single call number which have been dummied out to a remote location because of pressure of space. Sets
of two linear feet or more are normally candidates for this method,
with variations dependent, of course, upon the individual library cir-
cumstance. There should be an inventory of the blends, in the form
of a list (Figure 27). A copy of this inventory should be in the
possession of the library staff member guiding the pulling of books
in the main bookstack area of the present building and his counter-
part in the new building should also have a copy of this inventory.

A large placard should be placed in the shelf at the precise point
in the classification (next to the dummy); this notice should be about
10" x 14" (Figure 28). The dummied out material is brought from
its location to the bookstack area the day before so that it is on
hand when the pulling of the books reaches that point. The book
truck is likewise labeled with a large placard (cf. Figure 29), indicating it to be a blend and indicating the call number of the set
or sets.

Figure 27

Move Planning Form

Inventory of blends

Call number	Extent in linear feet	Location

The library staff member in the present building bookstacks has two guides to the imminence of a blend, the placard on the shelf, jutting out from the shelf for good visibility, and the inventory of blends (Figure 27). Check and re-check should be carried out to assure conformity between the inventory and the placards; the dummies should be checked as well to ascertain that none have been overlooked.

Figure 28

Sign for placement in bookstack

	B L E N D [Call number] [Extent, lin. ft.] [Location]

Figure 29

Sign for booktruck

B L E N D
[Call number] [Extent] [Location]

When the "blend" booktruck arrives in the bookstack area and
the last book preceeding the blend has been loaded onto the move
booktruck, the blend materials are emptied from the blend booktruck
to the move booktruck and the placard which signaled the blend is
discarded. It is important to transfer the books on the blend book
trucks to the move booktruck.

Method 3: Where a set or long run is located in another building
or where it is not practicable to blend.

Method 4: This concerns a large set or long run under a single
call number located in another building or where it is not practicable
to blend with the major group. It is necessary here to have a placard inserted in the present building main bookstacks at the point
where the set would normally be shelved. (Figure 30). This indicator cites the call number, extent in linear feet of the material
and, most important, the number of sections to be left vacant to receive this material when it reaches the new building. The placard
is moved with the books in its regular shelving order, and constitutes a directive to the shelvers in the new building. A register
or inventory of the sets to be handled under this procedure should
be compiled (Figure 31). This inventory gives the number of sections to be left empty. Accordingly, if books were being shelved at
1 booktruck: 1 section (i.e., 9.7 linear feet of books per section)
we would reserve a section as vacant if the set totalled from 8 to
12 linear feet.

Figure 30

Indicator to designate number of Sections to be left empty
(Method 4)

| L E A V E |
| S E C T I O N S |
| E M P T Y |
| [Call number] |
| [Extent, linear feet] |
| [Location] |

Figure 31

Move Planning Form

Inventory of sets and decision on number of empty
sections

Call number	Extent in linear feet	Location of books	Sections to be left empty

Method 5: This method is used for material concentrated in a
particular sub-class located in another building or when it is not
practicable to blend with the major group. It is sufficiently extensive such that provision is necessary. The measures taken for
such material is to leave sufficient sections completely empty when
we reach the classification point in shelving in the new building.

Which sections should be designated as empty? The best arrangement is to designate the empty sections on a pattern basis, since
the material to be handled under this method is not in the form of
sets of multi-volume works concentrated around a single call-num-
ber but is spread throughout a sub-class. If the major group of
Class HC is on the order of 900 linear feet and, as stated, the
minor group is on the order of 100 feet, we would want to have
our pattern to be on the order of every 10th section left empty. A
placard should be inserted to indicate the empty sections (Figure
32).

Transportation of booktrucks between buildings

The transportation of the booktrucks, if the present and new
buildings are close together, may be achieved by pushing the booktrucks. Otherwise a van or flatbed truck should be used. The NLM
move used a van with a capacity of 60 booktrucks, arranged in rows

Figure 32

Indicator to designate empty Section (Method 5)

indicator for

```
  E  M  P  T  Y           S  E  C  T  I  O  N
                      FOR
       SUB     —     CLASS  [                    ]

         TO  BE  MOVED  FROM
         [                                       ]
```

of 6 and columns of 10 each. Transit time was 50 minutes from
present to new building. In the UCLA move the flatbed truck used
15 booktrucks in rows of 3 and columns of 5. Transit time was approximately 7 minutes. In the NLM move, 2 vans were in use for
most of the book move; one sufficed in the UCLA move.

The booktrucks should be tied or secured in the van or flatbed
truck to prevent sliding and possible loss of books, especially if
the truck has to traverse rough roads.

The booktrucks going into the van will be in approximate order
by virtue of their loading. Exact order is unnecessary. On unloading the van, the arrangement on the loading dock in exact order is
not necessary. The trucks can be placed in order in the "staging
area" on the stack floor; arrangement of the booktrucks in numerical order on the loading platform may delay the loading of the van
with empty booktrucks for return to the old building.

Operations in the new building book stacks

The loaded booktrucks should be brought to the stack floor as
soon as possible after the van has brought them to the new building, and then arranged in numerical order in a "staging area" near
the area to which they relate. Normally, we might view the booktruck proceeding to the section and being unloaded; however, at
both the NLM and UCLA moves it was found expedient to make an
intermediate change, that is, the books on each fully loaded booktruck were transferred to the top shelf of three "transfer" booktrucks. It was found that books could be shelved more rapidly in

this manner, duplicative as the work seems, the reason being that the normal aisle makes unloading the three shelves of a single booktruck a time-consuming task.

Working with the method of one booktruck to one section, truck number 675 would simply have its books transferred to three "transfer" trucks; the placard would go on the first of the three transfer trucks. Assuming the correspondence method had, at a particular time, a ratio of 7:6, i.e., 7 booktrucks to every 6 sections, the same procedure would hold, namely, each of the seven booktrucks would result in 3 transfer trucks. The loading of the books into the sections would be guided by pre-numbering the sections with a sign. Thus, truck 675 through 681 would go into 6 sections; the first of the 6 sections would be marked with a sign "675."

The transfer booktruck procedure would work as well for the stacking formula in which we did not have one-to-one or other correspondence between booktruck and section.

Empty booktrucks are removed to a staging area to await the return of the next van or truck; booktrucks are then brought to the loading platform for placement on the van.

Working with the correspondence method of one booktruck per section, we can conveniently preassign the booktrucks to sections. For example, in beginning the shelving of the first stack floor in the new building the booktrucks would bear placards numbered 1, 2, 3, etc. The sections to which these booktrucks are to go can then be determined by simply counting the sections, by-passing those sections which, by design, are to be left empty for growth purposes. The preassignment of the booktruck number to the section does not necessarily mean that each section be given the booktruck number; it is satisfactory, for example, to indicate the booktruck number on, say, every fifth section. The main idea is to ensure the proper correspondence between booktrucks and sections.

It is undesirable to pre-assign the booktruck numbers to the sections too far ahead of the shelving operations. The reasons for this are: we may want to change our stacking formula from 1:1 to 7:6, which would force cancellation of the preassignments. Also, we may

receive an instruction in the form of a placard from the present
building which directs that 2 sections be left vacant (to accommodate 20 linear feet of Class B material which is stored in another
building and will be delivered next week).

The pre-assignment of booktruck numbers to the sections may be
examined if we do, in fact, make the change to a stacking formula
of 7:6. Suppose we have completed the shelving of booktruck 215 at
the 1:1 ratio and now are scheduled to use the 7:6 ratio. The seven
booktrucks bearing numbers 216 through 223 are shelved in the next
6 sections, etc. Again, if any sections are to be left vacant they
are bypassed in the numeration.

As soon as we determine the section at which the 7:6 ratio is
to begin, we place a sign in the section reading "Begin 7:6 ratio
here. " When booktruck 216 arrives and is ready to initiate the 7:6
ratio, placard 216 (which was on the booktruck) is marked with
fluid marking pencil "Begin 7:6 ratio" and is placed on the left-
hand side of the shelf of the first shelf to be used in that section.

A new placard reading "End Booktruck 223 at 7:6" is prepared
and placed on the right hand side of the last shelf in the sixth
section. Thus, we have two placards indicating the beginning and
ending points for the contents of the 7 booktrucks shelved in the 6
sections.

Spacing the books on the shelf

Under the ratio method of booktruck to section there is no need
for precision since the placement of the books is predicated on a
certain relationship of booktrucks to sections: this may be 1:1, or
7:6, or some other ratio. Once the ratio has been decided the
placement of the books on given shelves can be approximately ad-
hered to in the moving operation.

A device to establish and guide these approximate readings can be
a sign or simply a piece of 2" x 4" lumber with the length in
inches marked on it in large letters. This would be used on the
top shelf of the section and sighted for all the shelves in that section. Only a few of each dimension are required because they can
be re-used easily.

Checking Progress

How can we check the progress of the move? When using the
ratio method we can get a sufficiently accurate reckoning for operating purposes by the following methodology. Inspection of the
Move Planning Form shown in Figure 33 will be helpful. When a
specific sub-class or class is completed the number of areas and
the number of sections remaining on the floor under consideration
can be checked. Assuming Class AC-BX is on our first floor, when
Class AE is completed a certain number of sections will remain
available and these are counted.

Returning to the UCLA example at the end of Class JQ, 493
sections remained. From Class JS through Class PB a total of
4,966 linear feet of books were to be moved. By recourse to the
Move Planning Form (Figure 33) using the 1:1 stacking formula
for 378 sections and the 7:6 stacking formula for 115 sections, the
remainder can be made to fit. A later check, calculated on the
same form, with 125 sections remaining and Classes PA and PB,
with a total of 1,250 linear feet remaining, indicated that 101 sections could be handled at 1:1 and 24 sections at 7:6.

The decision to change the stacking formula should be made on
the basis of the outcome of the calculation set out in this Move
Planning Form. As the shelving approaches the end of the stack
floor it is desirable to proceed with a 1:1 ratio, since this will
give the better maneuverability in ending with the sub-class planned.

In the last few ranges of the last area of the floor, a special
maneuver is necessary. According to our plans, we intend a certain
class or sub-class to terminate a specified stack floor in the new
building. When the truck, bearing the last volume of the sub-class
of our intended termination has been placed on the truck, the truck
number is to be communicated immediately to the new building.
This is most important. This informs the new building shelvers of
the last number and permits final adjustment in the stacking formula,
if necessary. It may be that the sub-class measures a bit more
than the estimates. The stacking formula can be increased for a
sufficient number of sections to 7:6, or as necessary. Also, com-

Move Planning Form
Calculation of Shelving Progress on Stack Floor

Figure 33

Stack Floor   Intended Classes

Date   Time

A. Inventory of Sections

    (1) Sections on this stack floor: _____

    (2) Minus: Sections to be left empty: _____

    (3) Revised Sections on this floor: _____

    (4) Minus: Sections to be left empty for
        mergers after main move.   _____

    (5) Net total sections available for main move _____

B. Measurement of books to be moved

    Total linear feet of subject classes intended for
    this floor   _____

C. Check on shelving progress following end of (Sub)
    Class_____

    1. Sections remaining following the end of (Sub)
        Class_____

Areas remaining	Sections available
	Total:
	Minus: Sections in A (4) which have not as yet been reached at this time in shelving operation.

    2. Book material remaining to be moved following end of
        (Sub) class_____

Class	Extent in linear feet

    3. Relationship of shelf space to book material following end of
        class_____

$$9.7x + 11.3(N - x) = \text{Linear feet book material}$$
$$9.7x + 11.3(\quad -x) =$$

$$x = \frac{\rule{2cm}{0.4pt}}{1.6} =$$

_____ sections can be filled at 9.7 LF each
_____ sections can be filled at 11.3 LF each

pletely empty sections can be designated throughout the last several
ranges. As a matter of fact, once the last truck number for a stack
floor is known the shelving in the new building can actually be worked concurrently from the reverse direction. This can be the case
because of the system of ascribing a correspondence between booktrucks and sections.

Can we use the same concept for checking progress if we do
not use the ratio method of booktruck to section? Yes. Once we
know where the specific sub-class has terminated in the new building we know how many sections remain. We also know how many
linear feet remain for shelving on that stack floor (derived from
our measurement of the sub-classes intended for placement on
that stack level).

Thus we can use the Move planning Form in Figure 33, using
the figures with which we are operating. If we are shelving at 10
linear feet per section, and have just concluded a given sub-class,
we will want to know how many sections we can fill at 10 linear
feet and how many sections at some other figure.

Production

The linear feet of books which can be pulled from the present
building stacks, transported to the new building, and shelved there
is difficult to establish. There are variant factors in individual
library situations.

Some of these factors are accessibility to the book stacks,
elevator access, size and experience of the labor force and nature
and amount of equipment used.

Within the context of the environment used as examples here,
an average daily production range of 125 to 200 booktrucks is possible for the pulling of books in the old building. Shelving would
normally be at about 75 percent of the pulling rate unless the ratio
method is used.

It is perhaps an axiom in the moving industry that the pace of
the move proceeds no more rapidly than the speed with which the
material is put away at the destination. Since the ratio method permits several shelving operations to proceed concurrently, this per-

mits the same speed for shelving as for pulling.

A production total of 150 booktrucks per day, for example, would mean an average of about 1,500 linear feet or approximately 15,000 volumes.

Cleaning and safeguarding the books

Books may be vacuum cleaned in the present building well in advance of move time. The tops of the books, the portion usually requiring the principal cleaning attention, are difficult to reach.

The books can conveniently be cleaned during the course of the move. The place for such cleaning is while the books are on the loading platform awaiting transportation to the new building. Here they can be cleaned. An air blower can be used (30 lbs. per square inch pressure). A blower was used during the NLM move and was moderately successful. It did remove surface dust but did not remove the more deeply embedded grit.

During the UCLA move an industrial vacuum cleaner with a bristle brush of about 1-1/2 inches was used with superior results. Average time was about one minute per booktruck, the same time as the blower in the NLM move. Another disadvantage of the blower is the health hazard; if a blower is used the operator ought to be equipped with a mask. The vacuum cleaner has a clear advantage on this point.

The move director or his assistants should periodically check the handling accorded the books and should see that procedures are carried out. Any carelessness in handling and placing the books on the booktrucks should be corrected.

The mover should plan to have some kind of tarpaulin or plastic covering for the loading docks in the present and new building as well as on the trucks while in transit, as a protection against possible water damage.

Working conditions and safety

Health and accident hazards should not be overlooked during the course of the move. When removing books from the shelves in the present building considerable dust may be encountered. Ventilation should be provided if at all possible. If this is not possible, masks should be provided to the personnel working in the stack area; in fact, these should be provided whether or not adequate ventilation exists. A supply of bottled water should be on hand in the bookstack areas of the present and new buildings. An electric fan for air circulation, especially in badly ventilated stack areas is necessary.

Accidents can take place during the course of a move; this is especially true when fatigue and pressure combine. It is important, then, to make arrangements, to make known what they are and where they are located. A good first aid kit should be on hand at various points.

Communications: present building to new building

Telephone communication between the present and new building is essential. There should be a telephone on each level of the new building in order that the library supervisor in the new building can be reached promptly. There will be a number of messages which have to be handled promptly. These will concern the progress of shelving in the new building: what point it has reached, when the last numbered booktruck for a given collection has departed from the present building, etc. The names and telephone numbers of key staff members should be posted in a conspicuous place close to the telephone. A walkie-talkie should be investigated as a practical means to achieve rapid communication between the points of operation.

A corollary problem also exists in the present building in an open stack library. Beginning on "M Day" the stack level on which the move begins will have to be closed to readers, or at least a segment of the floor would have to be closed. Books could be paged from the entire or partial floor on which the move operations are proceeding. But this is a reasonable limitation to service during the move.

The problem, both in the present building (while it is the center of operations) and in the new building a bit later (when it is the center of operations) consists in tying up elevators.

Preparation of furniture and equipment for the move

The mover (professional mover, or buildings and grounds staff
member) in company with a library staff member appointed by the
Move Director will survey the individual library departments to assure that items to be moved have been adequately marked regarding location in the new building.

Grease pencil used on masking tape is a good method to prepare labels; such labels should be on the top of desks, backs of
chairs, tops of files, and on front of top shelf of bookcases. All
fragile equipment should be labeled clearly as such. Supply cabinets are moved empty; the supplies are preferably placed in large
wooden boxes. All boxes should be packed so they can be stacked.
Boxes and packages should not be of excessive weight. As previously noted, the small reference collections of books are to be transported by booktrucks, avoiding their packing in boxes or cartons.

Correspondence file cabinets can be transported with their files
and the files transferred in the new building by staff members. The
empty file cabinets are returned to the present building. This avoids
the packing of correspondence into boxes or cartons; the old correspondence file cabinets are actually containers in this sense.
The contents should be compressed toward the front of the cabinet
prior to moving. Such files can be locked.

Each library department should have one staff member in charge
at the present building and also in the new building. The identity of
such staff members should be made clear to the movers. It is important that furniture and equipment be routed quickly to its proper
place in the new building to avoid bottlenecks. Thus, the library
staff member in charge of the moving of furniture and equipment
at the new building has to know precisely the location for all items
and should be able to direct the proper disposition of the moved material quickly and accurately.

The transfer of cards from old to new trays

The number of cards has already been clearly marked by guide
cards in the present trays and the new cabinet trays should have the
new labels inserted. The transfer operation should take place as

close as possible to the new cabinets and a systematic work flow
arrangement devised so that there is a good pattern of flow. The
numbering of the guide cards permits the concurrent transferring of
cards by the Catalog Department staff members.

The appropriate number of staff members to use in concurrently
making the transfer of cards to the new trays will have to be determined on the basis of a number of considerations. The number
of movers engaged in pulling the trays from the old cabinets and
the size and frequency of the shipments of trays to the new building are the factors to be considered. If the cabinets can be transported with trays in them, this may result in a more productive
transportation schedule.

The UCLA public card catalog comprising 2,988 trays was transferred in two full days; actually, the transfer could have been completed in less time if the transportation of trays had been more frequent.

Chapter VI

Administrative Organization,

The Chronology of Operations and the Master Move Plan

Purpose

The purpose of the present chapter is to describe the administrative requirements involved in the move planning as well as in
the execution of the move. The role of the move director is discussed, as is the function of the move committee in providing information and relaying it to the staff. The need for staff studies to
support move planning is also covered.

The second portion of the chapter deals with a chronology of
events leading to the preparation of the master move plan; the
chronology recapitulates briefly the many items and actions presented in previous chapters, the intent to integrate them and to
state them in terms of a time schedule.

The administrative considerations

The move director is the principal administrative officer for the
entire move operation, with authority for final decision-making on
all aspects of the move. He is responsible for reporting of progress
and status of plans to the director of libraries. The move director
must have assistance in handling the varied issues involved in a
move. This assistance can be categorized as staff and line assistance. The principal staff assistance is a Move Committee, composed of representatives of the several departments of the library.

The Move Committee fulfills a number of important functions and
the interrelated character of the various departments' work makes
representation from all departments highly desirable.

The Committee serves to keep the move director informed of the
departmental needs with regard to the move; the committee advises
the move director of special problems, priorities, and work on
hand. The Committee also serves as the channel of information to

168

the staff regarding the nature and schedule of the move plan.

Since the structure of libraries will differ, it is desirable to indicate that the composition of the move committee be such that all
processes in the library which will affect and be affected by the
move be represented. Thus, for example, the catalog department
requires representation since the very important transfer of the
card catalog will be involved; the planning and inter-relationship of
this operation to the entire move is an important one.

Similarly, the reference department and the circulation department must also be represented since the matter of service to
clientele is involved both while the present building remains the
center of operation and until some time in the future when the new
building becomes the center of operations.

The relationship of equipment is important not only for the planning involved, but also in terms of timing or scheduling to fit in
with the other operations of the library. Thus, the representation
must take into consideration the needs of individual departments as
well as the interrelationship of the entire operation. Each of the
representatives should have an alternate if at all possible.

The frequency of meetings of the move committee should be dependent upon the needs of the move director and the planning requirements. When decisions have been made on substantive items,
they can be written up as "move memoranda" and issued to the
move committee. Such items might comprise the agreed upon arrangement of the collections in the new building; another might be
the announcement of the housecleaning operation to retire unneeded
equipment and supplies. The move memoranda, then, are designed
to acquaint the committee with the decisions or reports. These
memoranda can then be utilized by the move committee members
to inform their staffs about the development of move planning.

On a less comprehensive scale, announcements regarding move
planning can be prepared for the library's house organ or information bulletin.

The move committee members ought to be able to volunteer pertinent information or recommendations concerning the entire move

and also to serve as a source of information and judgment for the
move director.

The move director, in the elaboration of plans, may wish certain work projects to be carried out, in connection with the move
planning; thus, he may assign one of the departmental representatives to prepare data on the measurement of the collections, the
growth rate experienced by the different collections, or the recording of information relating to the transfer of cards from present
to new card trays, to mention only a few examples. Alternatively,
he may assign such a project, through its committee representative, to someone in the department. Such staff studies represent
an important part in move planning, and must be programmed or
scheduled with care and on an orderly basis. The move director
will appoint certain persons to carry out his decisions and entrust
them with certain decision-making authority.

The size and complexity of the move determines the number of
assistants required. The move director could simply have an assistant whose function would be to carry out decisions and act within the limits of certain lines of authority defined by the move director. The area of the book collections, covering their measurement, determination of their growth rate, etc., and the later direction of the moving of the collections, could reasonably form the
area of one of the move director's assistants. Another broad area
of assignment could be the furniture and equipment (including the
card catalogs, serial records, etc.). A third broad area would
represent the new building; here the person could plan the job of
monitoring the inflow of new equipment and furniture, keeping check
on the readiness of the various parts of the new building, etc.

For the actual moving operation, a moving cadre will have to
be formed, in some depth, to provide for the details of managing
the movement of the books, furniture and equipment. There will
have to be a library officer in charge of the present building, giving general direction and supervision to the movement of book materials as well as the non-book materials and a counter-part operation requires another library officer to assume direction and super-

vision at the new building.

The chronology of events and the master move plan

The nature, extent, and complexity of the individual library move will vary from library to library. There are, nonetheless, certain actions which will have to be taken in all of them. What is presented here is a chronology of events, stating month by month the facts, issues, events, plans, etc. which require consideration and solution. Although it is impossible to present a chronology that will meet the detailed needs of all libraries the chronology is designed to present the important issues. These are arranged in a sequence, indicating when they should be taken up in the order of time. The timing presented is not ironclad. It attempts to insert the various events and actions into a coherent plan, but individual library requirements can and will dictate refinements or amendments to the chronology.

The purpose of the chronology is to present the problems which will most probably have to be faced; to present them in terms of a schedule in which they might best be taken up, and to interrelate them. Another purpose in presenting the chronology is to provide a check list. The chronology presented assumes a large move and thus covers a twelve month period; this can readily be compressed for smaller moves. The form of the chronology is an outline; in certain parts it raises questions for checking, re-states certain important aspects for confirmation. The chronology for each month is organized around four headings: the present building; the new building; move operation; and administration.

Chronology of Events -First Month
Administration

(1) Preliminary meetings:- Series of preliminary meetings between director of libraries and his assistants. Discussions of general considerations of the move, probable date of new building completion, function of present building after the move, changes in library policy, thoughts on new and alternative arrangement of the collections, possible reorganization of the library based on new environment.

(2) Move director:- Appointment of move director by director of
libraries, elaboration of lines of authority by director of libraries--
what is expected, nature and extent of reporting by move director
to the director of libraries.

(3) Staff of the move director:- Based on size and complexity of
move, the designation by the move director of his principal as-
sistant(s). Designation may be on part time or full time basis with
specification of work area for which assistant is responsible or
without such specification at this time. Discussion on possible formation of move committee by move director. Description of the
new building and the move problem in general terms.

Chronology of Events - Second Month
Present Building:

(1) Present building condition:- General review and inspection of
the present building as a physical plant. The number and location
of elevators and their condition; the need for repairs to be noted.
Identification of the main aisles or corridors for moving purposes
with respect to the location of the loading platform(s). Traffic problems which appear likely. Does there appear to be need for an alternate elevator (i.e., portable outside elevator connecting with
windows) and loading platform?

(2) Furniture and equipment to be moved:- General plans regarding the moving of furniture and equipment to be moved to
the new building; provisional identification of problems with respect to heavier and larger furniture and equipment. Will any of
the present bookstacks be moved to the new building?

(3) Book collections to be moved:- General review of the book
collections, their condition, arrangement, characteristics, notation
of any special considerations. Will part or all of the book collections
be moved? Location of the various book collections should be noted.
Check should be made of storage areas and their location. Will
other campus libraries be merged with the main collection? Do the
books need cleaning? Does there exist a problem of insect infestation? Will remedial measures be required?

New Building:

(1) New building data:- What are the general facts and figures regarding the new building? Size, location, and function of the new building and the estimated capacity (number of sections) for books? What is the probable date for completion of the new building? Are there any problems which may alter this date significantly?

(2) New furniture and equipment needs:- What are the needs for new furniture and equipment for the new building and what is the status of planning for this? Has the requisition or order been prepared?

Administration

(1) The principal planning agencies and communication:- The names and function of the principal offices or agencies with which the library's move director will be working should be recorded; purpose here is to have clear understanding of the areas of work affecting the new building, present building, and the move per se, and the persons responsible for such areas, and to establish formal liaison with them. (Such offices, for example, might be the construction engineer, various suppliers, office responsible for issuance of invitations to bid, the buildings and grounds department, etc.)

(2) Arrange to have duplicated the move planning forms necessary to work out the various measurements, etc.

Chronology of Events- Third Month
Present Building:

(1) Book collections:- Examination of the book collections should be conducted without, at this point, beginning of formal inventory or measurement. The examination should be directed toward the nature of the collections, e.g., the need for special care on rare book materials, the approximate extent of special materials, such as microfilms, prints, maps, charts, etc. Will all or part of the collections be moved to the new building; if only a part will be moved, has a determination been made of the collections or classifications which will remain? What are the principles and issues involved in the division? Will the collections to be moved require mergers, or will a collection be split up. Here consideration should be given to

ways and means to arrange the collections in the new building in
a superior method. Finally, are there book materials stored in
other buildings and will these have to integrate with the main group
of books to be moved?

Measurement of the book collections in terms of linear feet of
book material, i. e. , using linear feet as standard of measurement
instead of volumes. Should a direct count be made, or is the collection of such large magnitude that a sampling be taken?

New Building:

(1) Visits to new building site:- Periodic visits to new building
site should be scheduled by the move director to inspect progress
of construction, determine if schedule appears to be met, check
location of entrances, etc. Notes should be taken of terrain between
present and new buildings (assuming two buildings close by) and
the condition of roads or other means of access.

Administration:

(1) Meetings of the move committee:- Meetings of the move committee should be scheduled on a periodic basis by the move director. Plans should be made by the move director to have discussion
of pre-designated topics in order to have members prepare data.
Brief record of substance of discussions or agreement on procedure, etc. should be planned.

(2) Planning room:- A planning room should be designated and
made available to the move director and his assistant. In this
planning room should be kept the relevant working materials bearing on the move, e. g. , the various drawings of the new building,
preferably in a cabinet to permit easy access, sufficient table
space for large drawings and charts, bulletin boards for posting
floor plans and stack drawings, blackboard or easel, Chart-Pak
material for indicating furniture and equipment layouts, fluid marking pencils, and other necessary supplies. Facilities and channels
for promptly obtaining photoreproductions of charts, plans and dia-
grams should also be established at this time.

(3) Documentation and communication:- Establishment of "move
memoranda" series should be considered; the move memoranda

would encompass basic steps in the move planning (e.g., survey
of furniture & equipment, announcement of move schedule, housecleaning program, etc.) for transmittal to department heads and
others concerned.

Copies of pertinent correspondence and other materials should
be directed to move committee members.

Chronology of Events-Fourth Month
Present Building:

(1) Study of the present building bookstack areas:- It is desirable
to prepare a map of the present bookstack areas, floor by floor,
to illustrate the number and location of ranges and showing sections.   This is important for later planning.

An inventory or tally of the number of bookshelves in the ranges
should be made; this counting should be accomplished in terms of
the individual collections, classifications, or sub-classifications
used in the library organization of the collections. The counting
will encompass all shelves in each single-faced range, and the
number of empty shelves in each single-faced range. The difference between all shelves and vacant shelves will give us non-empty
shelves, an important figure for the later measurement of the size
of the collection. A similar procedure should be utilized at this
same time for the bookshelves containing reference materials in
the various reading rooms. In addition, an inventory should be
planned for the unbound issues of periodicals displayed in reading
rooms.

New Building:

(1) Study of the new building bookstack areas:- An enlarged copy
of the new building plans, illustrating the bookstack areas, should
be procured. Using the bookstack plans as a basis a tally should
be made of the number of single-faced ranges and the number of
sections. It is desirable, at this point, to designate the areas by
letters or numbers; normally, this designation will proceed in the
same order as the sequence of shelving. If the sequence of shelving
has not as yet been determined, the areas can be given a provisional
designation, which is merely to identify them for the purpose of in-

ventory. Totals should be given for the various levels or floors.

A similar study should be conducted of the reading room shelves to determine capacity; in addition, a measurement should be made of the capacity of the shelves which will house display issues of periodicals in the reading rooms.

Move From Present to New Building

(1) Preliminary study of the transporation of furniture and book materials to the new building:- Attention and discussion should be directed toward the matter of manpower in the actual moving operation. Will this represent staff involvement in the actual physical work and to what extent? Will the services of a professional mover, or the buildings and grounds department be used? Another arrangement to be considered is use of the professional mover or buildings and grounds department in handling the physical aspects of the move, with library staff participation being limited to directing the pulling of books from the shelves and their placement in the new building. The moving of furniture and equipment will presumably be handled by outside labor, a professional moving concern or the buildings and grounds department.

A corollary to this study is the matter of what method of transporting books should be used, whether boxes, cartons, booktrucks, or book carts are to be used. The mobility given by use of book carts should be given serious attention. The question of the number of book carts or boxes, etc., should be determined, at least in approximate terms, since the question of procuring the necessary quantity at a specific time may require negotiation.

Administration

(1) Progress report to the staff:- News notes regarding the move planning should be prepared for the library's information bulletin. It is also desirable to have a meeting, depending on the size of the library move and its complexity, at a few times during the course of the move planning to assure that fully adequate information is imparted to the staff. These meetings can be conducted by the move director with the department heads who can, in turn, inform their staffs; alternatively, it may be desirable to have the move director

hold a meeting which will be attended by the entire staff. Or there
may be a combination of the two methods of imparting information.
Such meetings should be for presenting decisions and determina-
tions, and there should be a period for questions. Desirably the
meetings should progressively provide a greater degree of detail.
As a general guide such meetings might be held at the end of the
fourth, eighth, and eleventh months.

Chronology of Events-Fifth Month

Present Building:

(1) Measurement of the book collections:- (Part 1) The total
number of occupied shelves will have been derived from the study
of the present building book stack areas (Fourth Month). From
these totals will be derived the total linear feet of shelving, normally the number of non-empty shelves multiplied by 3 linear feet
but with variation if shelves are of varying interior dimension. The
sampling will be based on the count of linear feet of non-empty
shelves for each collection, classification, or sub-classification as
desired. This process of measurement should be initiated during
the current month and completed by the end of the sixth month.

The measurement of the size of reference collections shelved
in the reading rooms may be calculated by the same method or by
a direct count if the collection is small. The measurement of the
unbound issues displayed in the reading rooms should be done by
counting the number of issues per shelf.

Study of the growth of the collections:- Data should be accumu-
lated for a study of the growth characteristics of the different parts
of the collections. Desirably these data should be in detailed form,
that is, in terms of the LC classification (or sub-classes) or in
terms of the arbitrary collection names in the given library. This
study should cover recent years (5 to 10 years), and consideration
should be given, in the analysis of such data, to whether the
growth during the period studied will be characteristic in the future.
Data will ordinarily be available in terms of volumes added to the
collections; there should be derived, then, a set of data which will
portray the percentage change from year to year for each classifi-

cation concerned. This percentage will then be applied to the data
on linear feet of material on hand. This will indicate the estimated
linear feet of book material added.

For the reference collections in the reading rooms a survey
should be made to ascertain if collections will be expanded, contracted, or remain the same for the new building's reading rooms.
The same holds true for the unbound issues of periodicals displayed
in the various reading rooms.

Chronology of Events-Sixth Month
Present Building:

(1) Measurement of the book collections:- (Part 2) Measurement
should be completed at the end of the month; there should exist
total linear feet figures for each of the collections, or classifications or sub-classifications.

(2) Study of rate of growth of the various collections:- (Part 2)
This study should also be completed at the end of the month and
should contain the percentage changes in the number of volumes from
year to year. There should be an average annual percent of change
for each classification or sub-classification.

New Building:

Planning the location of departments and divisions:- The basic building plans may set forth the location of the various departments, at
least in a broad sense, without exact location of desks, equipment,
bookshelves, etc. It will remain for the move director to assure
himself that the detailed planning of this sort is reviewed at this
point and to determine the final placement of equipment and furniture.

Chronology of Events-Seventh Month
Present Building:

(1) Survey of furniture and equipment:- A survey should be conducted during the month to inventory the furniture and equipment
to be moved to the new building. This should be carried out by department on the basis of an instruction setting up the procedures.
Furniture and equipment should be color-coded with stickers to in-

dicate the floor and room number in the new building; in addition, a summary form (inventory) of such materials should be prepared for the convenient use of the moving organization, to estimate the magnitude and relative difficulty of the job.

It will be desirable to plan the disposition of furniture and equipment which will not be moved. Will it remain in the present building or will it be disposed of to other offices or agencies? Furniture and equipment which is not to be moved to the new building and which is not currently in use may be conveniently tagged for early disposition, simply to clear the decks for the move.

The Moving Operation

(1) The nature of staff participation:- Final decision should be taken as to the involvement of staff manpower, on the assumption that the staff will participate only to the extent of supervising the movement of the book collections. The requirements for library staff manpower in this context is still considerable and planning should proceed toward the designation of staff members who will exercise this function. Persons selected should be responsible and should know the shelving order of the collections in the present building and the planned sequence in the new building. Alternates should be nominated as well. In addition, there should be one library staff member in the present building and in the new building as the responsible library officer in immediate charge. This should be a higher level supervisor, again with alternate. After the naming of the persons responsible they should be briefed as to move plans concerning their immediate responsibilities. Additional library personnel will be required to direct the moving of furniture and equipment, card catalogs, reference materials from the reading rooms, etc.

The library move organization should be thoroughly briefed on the move plans, and kept informed of move planning from this time forward, and during the Tenth Month there should be a test move.

Chronology of Events-Eighth Month

Moving Operation

Inventory of book trucks, book carts, etc.:- If book trucks are
to be used in the move it is necessary to take a careful inventory
of the number of booktrucks on hand and to ascertain the number
which will be directed to the moving operation. Booktrucks which
are not essential to regular working operations should be designated.
Cognizance may be taken of the possibility of borrowing booktrucks
from other libraries, but this should normally be considered an
emergency measure.

Numbered placards for booktrucks:- Cardboard placards should
be prepared, measuring approximately 10" x 14"; numerals are to
be marked with grease pencil or fluid marker on both sides of
placard.

Administration

Progress report to the staff;- A report to the staff along the
lines described in the Fourth Month should be held.

Present Building:

Duplicates and exchange material:- A schedule should be worked
out so that duplicates and exchange material can be disposed of
prior to the move to spare the expense of moving such material to
the new building. Similarily, plans should be established such that
no inordinate amounts of exchange material are acquired prior to
the move.

Insecticiding present building bookstack areas:- A study should be
made of the incidence of insect infestation and remedial action taken
at the prescribed time if required.

New Building

Trial "arrangement" of the collections:- Data needed at this point
consist of the measurement of the collections expressed in linear
feet, the growth percentages of the various classifications, and the
data on the capacity of the new bookstack areas. First, the growth
percentages can be applied to the estimated size of the collection
(linear feet) and projections derived which will indicate the estimated size of the collections for a number of years ahead. Thus,
the adequacy of certain areas in the new building can be tested for

specific classifications. Provisional layouts on an enlarged chart of
the new bookstack areas can be indicated with fluid marking pencil.
The limit of the new building areas will prescribe the outer limits
of growth space to be provided, but adequate growth space should
be "built into" the placement. How the growth space will be provided relates to the stacking formula, that is, the percentage of
each section to be filled with books. Provisional layouts should be
made with stacking formulas in mind, and given areas inspected
from the standpoint of capacity, additional space to be interspersed,
etc. In a closed stack library attention ought to be directed to the
placement of the more used collections near the elevator or left.

This trial placement should be initiated during the current month
and completed, in final form, by the end of the Ninth Month.

Chronology of Events- Ninth Month

Administration

Staff visit to new building:- This is intended to familiarize the
staff with the new environment, to inspect future library quarters,
and to have a question and answer period with respect to the new
building. The tours should be conducted by the move director or
his alternate.

New Building

Arrangement of the collections:- As a result of the trial arrangements initiated during the previous month, a final decision should be
made by the end of the current month of the placement of the collections in the new building areas. This arrangement will be useful
for rapidly preparing a new "directory of the collections"--a document which will be very useful for staff and users in the new building.

Move Operation

The nature of the job for the mover:- On the basis of the planning to date it is necessary to set down, in provisional form, what
will be expected of the move organization (whether it be a professional mover or local labor supply). Such description should indicate
the tentatively selected moving date, the estimated duration of the

move, the amount of furniture, equipment, and book materials,
and the extent and manner in which library staff personnel will
participate in the moving.

Moving Operation

(1) Test or simulated move:- During the month a day should be
reserved for a test of the move plans. This will include the pulling
of volumes from one of the present building bookstack areas, loading them onto book trucks, book carts or other means of transport), the loading of the book trucks onto a moving van. The placement of the books onto the new bookshelves can be simulated by
returning the volumes to their shelves in the present building. This
test will, of course, provide useful data on the move route, the
elevator, loading platform and relative speed in pulling books from
shelves, placing them on book trucks and the reverse operation.
Variations of the test will be determined by the nature of the move,
the location of the new building, and other factors. It is, however,
important to have a test at this stage in order to examine the
plans in operation. A benefit of the test, as well, is that it will
bring up problems which may not have been covered in the planning.
It is important to time the various operations as a guide toward
the actual move itself. The physical labor during the test may have
to come from library staff, unless arrangements can be made with
the moving organization which will be responsible for the final
move. Time spent on various operations should be recorded with a
stop watch, e.g., the time to load a booktruck, the time to push
the truck to the elevator entrance, the time waiting for the elevator,
time on the elevator, the time from elevator exits to loading platform, and the time involved in getting the booktruck positioned on
the moving van. The averages for these separate operations as well
as the total average time from bookstack to moving van should also
be secured.

Present Building:

Housecleaning:- Plans should be formulated for a systematic

housecleaning of the present building which should occur at the end
of the month. The purpose of the housecleaning is to divest the library of unneeded supplies, records, and miscellaneous material
to avoid the time, effort, and expense of moving it to the new
building. The procedure can be described in a move memorandum
and it is most desirable that an inspection schedule be established
in accordance with which the move director, with the department
head, will make an inspection to determine the nature and extent
of the housecleaning.

Administration

Re-check of figures and data:- It is essential at this point to
review the data in order to check on its accuracy. Such validation
should cover the measurement of the collections, the determination
of the growth rate, the provision for growth in the new building
areas including the stacking formulas, as well as the placement
of the collections to determine adequacy of the arrangement.

Move Operation

Inspection of the building by the mover:- If the moving is to be
handled by a professional moving concern and if the contract is to
be awarded on a bid basis, it is necessary that the professional
movers make an examination of the present and new buildings to
familiarize themselves with what is to be moved, the difficulties inherent in the job, etc., as a basis for their bid formulation. Such
an open house should involve a presentation by the move director
of move plans as formulated to date, and tour of the present and
new buildings, followed by a question and answer period.

Chronology of Events-Eleventh Month

Administration

Communication between present and new building:- It is essential
that a telephone line be in operation between the present and new
building by the end of the twelfth month at the very latest. It is
mentioned at this time so that adequate time exists for having this
accomplished. There should be a telephone instrument on each
level of the new building, since it is important that the library of-

ficer in charge of moving operations in the new building can be reached immediately. There should also be phones at both loading platforms and each station should have a list of key phone numbers conspicuously posted.

Move Operation

Collaboration and planning with the mover:- The mover should be designated at the beginning of the month and a series of planning conferences should be initiated. These discussions should refine the planning and spell out responsibilities.

Administration

Provision of guard service for security purposes:- Plans should be drawn up for the provision of suitable guard service to maintain the security of rare books during the move and security provision for the materials in the new building during the move.

Present Building

Summary on present building readiness:- Careful check should be made on readiness of book collections for the move, items such as completion of mergers, arrangements for special materials (rare books, fragile materials, maps, folios, microfilm, etc.)

Move Operation

Sequence of moving:- The order in which various collections are to be moved into the new building should be firmly established. This may follow classification order or may be based on moving least used materials first.

Sequence of moving departments and their equipment, etc.:- Decision on the sequence in which the various departments and their furniture, equipment, work in progress, etc. will be moved should be made. Generally, technical processes should be moved first, followed by public services. Move of public services including reference collections, public card catalog, should occur just prior to changeover.

Manpower and equipment:- Check should be made of the moving cadre, alternates, readiness of move organization, knowledge of procedures and the overall move plan. Check should also be made

as to the adequacy of the supply of book trucks, book carts, or
other moving equipment to be utilized.

New Building

Readiness of new building:- Check should be made on completion
date of new building, and its acceptance by the appropriate authority. The date, if different than that planned will require revisions
in time schedules. New building readiness should be checked as to
elevators, loading platforms, book stacks, etc. Deliveries of new
furniture and equipment, placement in designated locations, status
of public card catalog delivery and placement, furniture for reading rooms, should also be subjected to checks and verifications of
schedule.

Administration

Formulation of the Master Move Plan:- A large number of factors have been considered in the chronology to date. At the beginning of the month these factors should be fitted into a master move
plan; this plan should be gradually refined and completed during the
twelfth month. Basically the master move plan sets out the final
order in which various interrelated move events are to take place,
prescribing the time schedule for completion of specific operations.
The plan is predicated on a number of dates: date on which the new
building is ready to receive book materials; second, the date on
which the move will begin; third, the determination of the changeover date, that is, the date on which the new building will become
the center of operations supplanting the present building in this
respect. The master move plan, then, seeks to build a series of
events around these dates. Basically, the master move plan sets
forth the move operation in terms of operations and time schedules,
and is the result of the planning and actions spelled out in this
chronology.

Chronology of Events-Twelfth Month
Administration

Progress report to the staff:- This meeting of the staff is along
the lines described for the fourth month (and eighth) but with the

added factor that the meeting can be utilized to outline some of the
procedures in the actual move. More time should be allowed for
questions here because the sense of imminence of the move will be
present for many staff members and it is desirable to provide firm
and unequivocal answers to questions.

Communications link between present and new building:- Telephone
line to assure communication between present and new building
should be in place between present and new building. Instruments
should be ready on each of the floors or levels in the new building.

Elaboration of the master move plan:- Refinement and necessary
amendment to the master move plan, begun during the previous
month, should continue. Dates, time schedules, should be restudied
to secure the best possible plan.

Present Building

Preparation for move of staff members' working materials:-
Toward the end of the month staff members should be provided
with cardboard cartons to hold miscellaneous in-desk and on-desk
items, except for book materials. Each box should be labelled with
staff members name, department, and room or level number in new
building. Work in progress -- at a minimum -- should be similarly boxed. The timetable for this step will vary, depending on the
department's move schedule. Having these materials boxed too early
means termination of regular work; doing this too late complicates
the move. The desk items and work in progress should be boxed
and sealed at the end of the day just before the department is
scheduled to be moved. Filing cabinets should be adjusted so that
correspondence is tightly packed; supply cabinets should be emptied
and their contents placed in cardboard containers which should then
be appropriately labeled. Miscellaneous card file cabinets should be
taped up to prevent drawers from falling out.

Equipment:- Photoduplication equipment, punched card equipment,
electric typewriters, etc. may require servicing by the manufacturer as part of a make ready operation for the move. The plans for
scheduling this should be made during the month, and arrangements
made in accordance with the particular move schedule of the given

department.

Present Building

Insecticiding of present building bookstack areas:- Treatment of book collections unless already undertaken should be completed during the month on the basis of thorough check by responsible authority.

Book cleaning:- If book collections are to be cleaned in transit arrangements should be completed to have on hand either air blower (effective for light surface dust) or a vacuum cleaner for more thorough cleaning. Plans should be made as to the location of this cleaning, whether loading platform or elsewhere, and staffing and equipment arrangements firmed up.

Parking restrictions: Instructions should be issued regarding the parking of automobiles at or near the loading platform during the move period.

Glossary of Terms

Area	A "cluster" or group of ranges surrounded by aisle space.
Actual capacity of an area	The total linear feet of shelving constituting an area.
Booktrucks	Conventional library booktruck of three shelves, approximately 36 inch interior shelves; also a set of three boxes, providing the same shelf dimensions, mounted on a dolly.
Center of operations	The transaction of normal library routines and services, -e.g., reference and circulation services, photoduplication services, and technical processes in a library building.
Changeover	Day on which moving operation has proceeded to the point that the new building, instead of the present building, constitutes the center of operations of the library.
Collection	A portion of the library's total holdings; a discrete LC class or sub-class, or a group of books designated by a particular label.
Collection of library materials	The total or aggregate holdings of the library including the volumes shelved in the reading room(s) and including the various forms of material (i.e., books, periodicals, newspapers, microfilms, maps, music scores, phonodiscs)
Density of shelving	The extent to which a shelf, section area, stack level is occupied by books. Greater density signifies more books per shelf, section, etc.; lesser density signifies less books per shelf, section, etc.
Dummied out volume	Volume or set of volumes shelved in location other than normal classification point and represented by wooden block indicating call number and location of given volume or set of volumes.

Empty shelf	Shelf completely vacant.
Growth space or expansion space	The space provided on the shelf, in the section, or in the range, or area, for the future growth of the collection.
Linear foot; linear inch	Standard of measurement used in the determination of the extent of shelf space and in computing the size of the individual collections.
Major group	In a merger, the numerically larger group of books into which the smaller is merged.
Merger, merging	Consolidation of two or more groups of books into a single arrangement.
Minor group	In a merger, the numerically smaller group of books which is merged into the larger group.
Move day or "M Day"	The beginning of the moving of library materials furniture and equipment from the present to the new building.
Mover	The non-library moving assistance provided either by professional moving company or by labor force from the university or the administrative organization of which the library is part.
New building readiness	The readiness of the new building to permit library materials, furniture and equipment, and staff to be moved into it. (This does not necessarily signify that the new building is totally completed.)
Non-empty shelf	Shelf occupied by some books.
Occupancy ratio	Linear feet of books divided by linear feet of shelf space.
Section occupancy ratio	The number of linear feet of books in a section divided by 21 linear feet (or whatever the computed actual capacity, which is dependent upon actual interior length of shelves), e.g.,

$$\frac{10.5 \text{ lin. ft. books}}{21.0 \text{ lin. ft. shelves}} = .50, \text{ occupancy ratio}$$

Floor (or stack level) occupancy ratio	The number of linear feet of books on a floor or stack level divided by the number

of linear feet of shelf space on the stack level.

Library occupancy ratio
The number of linear feet of books in the library's stack areas divided by the number of linear feet of shelf space in its stack areas.

Order of shelving
The sequence followed in shelving a collection within a section, within the single-faced range, and from one area to another.

Practical capacity of an area
The total linear feet of shelving which is usable; 75 to 80 percent of the actual capacity represents the practical capacity. (75 percent would represent the point at which the shelving of newly acquired book materials is difficult.)

Section
A vertical arrangement of shelves, normally consisting of a base shelf and six adjustable shelves of approximately 35 inch interior length.

Shelf
Shelf approximately 36 inches in interior length.

Shelving sequence
The order decided upon for the arrangement of books from range to range and from area to area.

Single-faced range
A row of sections, variable as to the number of sections contained therein.

Stacking formula
The number of linear feet of books in the individual section and the ratio to the section capacity (normally 21 lin. ft.); includes also the arrangement, i.e., the designation of empty shelves and fractional occupancy of other shelves in the section.

Ratio method
The ratio between booktruck and section, e.g., 1 booktruck: 1 section indicating that the contents of one booktruck are shelved in one section; 7 : 6 indicating contents of 7 booktrucks go to 6 sections.

Non-ratio method
No ratio between booktruck and section, books are placed in sections on the basis of desired number of linear feet per shelf and section.

Staff occupancy of the   The date on which the staff assumes its
new building   duties in the new building, usually concur-
                          rently with changeover; although staff oc-
                          cupancy may occur in stages, by depart-
                          ments or divisions.

Statistical Appendix

This section provides background and an analysis of the technique of measurement. In that technique sampling procedures may be used to estimate the extent, in linear feet, of books on library shelves. In the present section certain of the statistical and probability characteristics of shelves and books are reviewed and an outline of the significance of the derived data is presented.

The objective of statistical inference is to permit generalization from a sample to some larger population of which the sample is a part and the problem in measuring books on shelves by sampling becomes one of determining how well we can infer the population from the sample. In our specific problem we have a population of X number of library shelves (normally 35.00 or 33.25 inches interior length) on which books are shelved. The density or closeness with which books are pressed together represents a problem in measurement. We have defined normal array where books are subject to compression exerted by a bookend, but there is error that depends upon intensity of compression.

The population mean is represented by the arithmetic mean of the number of linear inches of book materials on X number of shelves; we do not know the parameters (measures descriptive of our population of shelves with books on them; but we can forecast the parameters from our sample statistics with known degrees of accuracy.

In order to secure a sample as randomly drawn as possible, a systematic sample was used at both the National Library of Medicine and UCLA moves. The initial shelf number was selected from a table of random numbers. The representativeness of the sample mean depends upon two characteristics of the distribution: (1) N, the number of cases, and; (2) the variability, or spread of scores around the mean.

The 280 samples yielded an arithmetic mean of 28.22 inches and a

192

Figure 34

DISTRIBUTION OF 280 SAMPLE MEASUREMENTS, NLM

	6.0 7.9	8.0 9.9	10.0 11.9	12.0 13.9	14.0 15.9	16.0 17.9	18.0 19.9	20.0 21.9	22.0 23.9	24.0 25.9	26.0 27.0	28.0 29.9	30.0 31.9	32.0 33.9	34.0 35.9
F	2	3	3	3	4	6	8	19	24	20	16	19	25	107	21

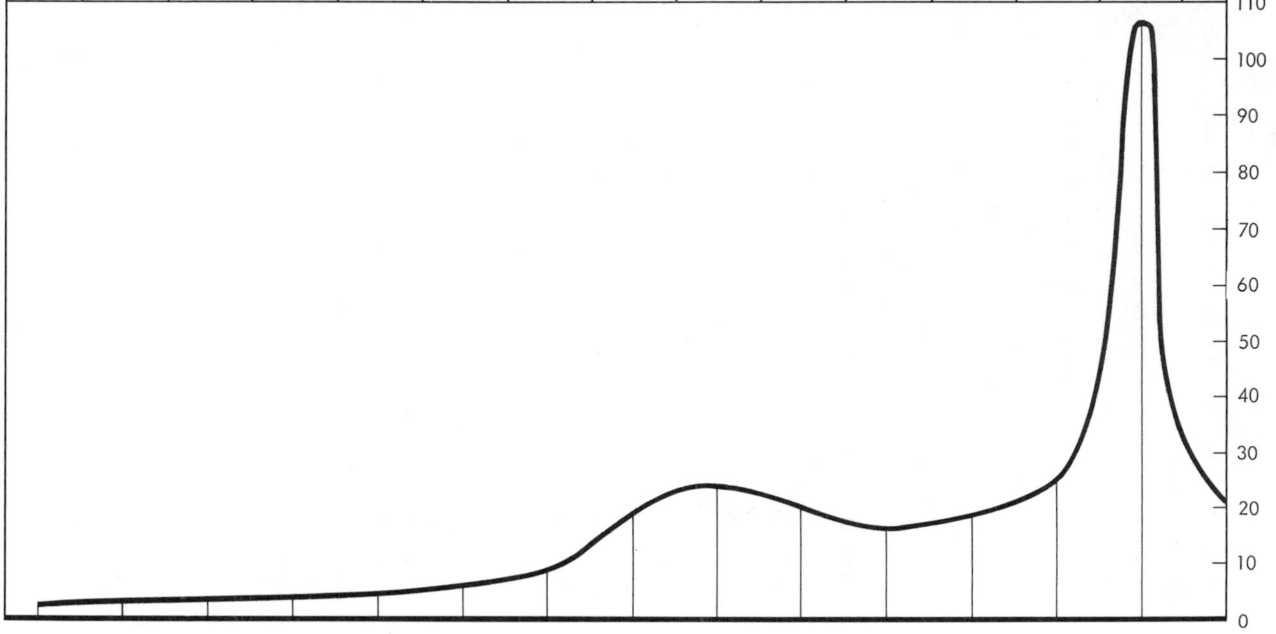

193

standard deviation of 6.1 inches the distribution is shown in the graph
(Figure 34).

We may make a number of observations at this point concerning
library shelves with books on them. The library shelves are (normally) of standard length (35.00 or 35.25 inches). We are interested in the population of such shelves containing books. First, the
possible range of occupancy of a given library shelf is covered by
stating that we can have from one book to many books -- from a
low of one book which may vary, say, from 0.25 inch (only one
small book) up to a high of many books, but up to a normal maximum of 35.00 or 35.25 inches. This is a statement of the extremes.
A library faced with the job of moving is obviously almost always
one in which the shelves are crowded, even extremely crowded.
This signifies that the variability or spread, linear inches of books,
should be concentrated in the higher reaches of this range (as in
Figure 34). In fact, we may assert that the variability would tend
to be quite small, with a very high number of cases in the higher
reaches of the shelf capacity, i.e., the 33.00 or 33.25 inch measurement.

Table 22 which follows provides various data if we assume an
estimated sample mean of 29.00 inches and a standard deviation
of 6 inches. Here we indicate the increased reliability we secure
by increasing the size of the sample (n). This will provide a guide
to the selection of the proper standard size given the requirement
for accuracy which it is felt is necessary in the given library situation.

Appendix

Figure 34a

Move Planning Form

Frequency Distribution Form
(Tally Sheet)

Class boundaries (Linear inches of books)	Tally	Frequency
1.75 — 3.75		
3.75 — 5.75		
5.75 — 7.75		
7.75 — 9.75		
9.75 —11.75		
11.75 —13.75		
13.75 — 15.75		
15.75 — 17.75		
17.75 — 19.75		
19.75 — 21.75		
21.75 — 23.75		
23.75 — 25.75		
25.75 — 27.75		
27.75 — 29.75		
29.75 — 31.75		
31.75 — 33.75		
33.75 — 35.75		

Figure 35

Move Planning Form

Frequency Distribution Form

Calculation of Mean and Standard Deviation for Measurement
of Books

Class boundaries (Linear inches of books)	Class mark	Number of shelves f	Coded mid-value m	f m	f m^2
1. 75 — 3. 75	2. 75				
3. 75 — 5. 75	4. 75				
5. 75 — 7. 75	6. 75				
7. 75 — 9. 75	8. 75				
9. 75 — 11. 75	10. 75				
11. 75 — 13. 75	12. 75				
13. 75 — 15. 75	14. 75				
15. 75 — 17. 75	16. 75				
17. 75 — 19. 75	18. 75				
19. 75 — 21. 75	20. 75				
21. 75 — 23. 75	22. 75				
23. 75 — 25. 75	24. 75				
25. 75 — 27. 75	26. 75				
27. 75 — 29. 75	28. 75				
29. 75 — 31. 75	30. 75				
31. 75 — 33. 75	32. 75				
33. 75 — 35. 75	34. 75				

Table 22

The standard error of the mean on the basis of estimated SD of 6" and an estimated mean of 29.00" illustrating size of sample (m) required to get specified variation from mean.

n	1	10	20	40	80	100	120	140	160	200
$SE_{mean} = \dfrac{SD}{\sqrt{n}}$	6	1.89	1.34	0.94	0.67	0.60	0.54	0.50	0.47	0.42
SE_{mean} X 1.96 SE	±11.76	±3.70	±2.62	±1.84	±1.31	±1.17	±1.05	±0.98	±0.92	±0.82
Percent Variation from an est. M of 29"	±40.55%	±12.75%	±9.03%	±6.34%	±4.51%	±4.03%	±3.62%	±3.37%	±3.17%	±2.82%

Number of volumes per linear foot

Table 23 indicates the number of volumes per linear foot arranged by LC subject class. In Figure 36 the data is shown in a histogram.

Table 23

Number of Volumes Per Linear Foot, Arranged by LC
Subject Class

Class	Number of books per foot
A	8.55
B	11.50
C	9.91
D	9.89
E	9.60
F	9.35
G	10.96
H	10.84
J	10.34
K	7.40
L	12.07
M	12.68
N	10.88
P	12.30
Q	10.95
R	11.73
S	10.12
T	9.67
U	9.28
V	10.81
Z	14.03
All Classes	10.78

Note: These data were developed as a by-product of the sampling process; the number of books in the first linear foot of the sample shelf was established and recorded. The compression exerted was that of a bookend after books had been evened on the shelf.

Figure 36

HISTOGRAM ILLUSTRATING DISTRIBUTION OF NUMBER OF VOLUMES PER LINEAR FOOT

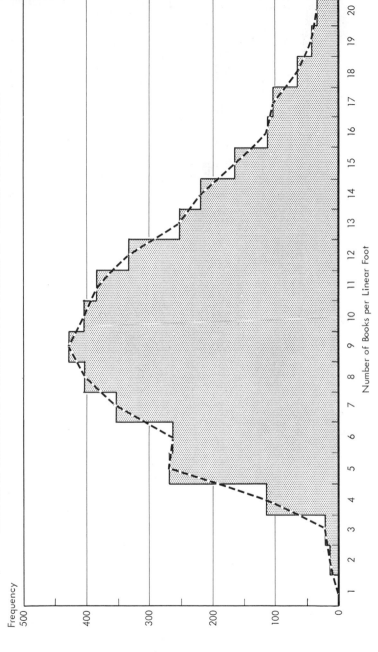

Table 24

Allocation of Subject Class to Floors of the University Research Library and Statistics on the Book Move

(Regular Size Books)

(1)	(2)	(3)	(4)	(5)	(6)	(7)	(8)
Class or Sub-Class assigned to floor	Estimates of book material (linear feet) to be moved	Floor location assigned in U.R.L.	Actual book material (linear feet)[1] moved	Estimated book material (linear feet)[2] to be added after main move	Total book material (linear feet) to be in U.R.L. by September 1964 (Col. 5 plus col. 6)	Number of sections on U.R.L. Floor specified[3]	Average occupancy in (linear feet) per section (linear feet) (Col. 6 divided by col. 7)
AC - BX	9,292	2	9,215	625	9,840	980	10.0
CB - HB	18,512	3	18,285	243	18,528	1,942	9.5
HC - PB	16,592	4	16,606	1,399	18,005	1,942	9.3
PC - Z	18,624	5	18,882	74	18,954	1,942	9.7
Totals	63,020	- - -	62,988	2,341	65,327	6,806	9.6

1. Indicates regular-size book material moved from Main Library (booktrucks x constant 9.7 lin.ft. per book truck).

2. Indicates book material from Institute of Industrial Relations and Graduate Reading Room, plus miscellaneous materials not listed on part of "primary move" in Cols. 2 and 4.

3. Included within the "available" sections are the sections equipped with reference shelves; in all cases these are left vacant for growth purposes (equivalent to leaving each 15th section vacant). Their number is: Floor 2('74); Floors 3 through 5 (133 each) or a total of 473 sections.

Table 25

Allocation of Subject Class to Floors of the University Research Library and Statistics on the Book Move

(Over Size Books)

(1) Class or Sub-Class assigned to floor	(2) Estimates of book material (linear feet) to be moved	(3) Floor location assigned in U.R.L.	(4) Actual book material (linear feet)[1] moved	(5) Estimated book material (linear feet)[2] to be added after main move	(6) Total book material (linear feet) to be in U.R.L. by September 1964 (Col. 5 plus col. 6)	(7) Number of sections on U.R.L. Floor specified[3]	(8) Average occupancy (in linear feet) per section (linear Feet) (Col. 6 divided by col. 7)
AC-DP	1263	3	1272	1	1273	120	10.6
DQ-HG	1149	4	1154	118	1272	120	10.6
HJ-Z	1257	5	1319	32	1351	120	11.2
Totals	3669	- - -	3745	151	3896	360	10.8

1. Indicates over-size book material moved from Main Library (booktrucks x constant 9.7 lin. ft. per book truck).
2. Indicates book material from Institute of Industrial Relations and Graduate Reading Room, plus miscellaneous materials not listed on part of "primary move" in Cols. 2 and 4.
3. Included within the "available" sections are the sections left vacant for growth purposes (each 15th section vacant). There are eight vacant sections on each of the floors.

Tables 24 and 25 indicate the arrangement of the collections in the University Research Library, UCLA. The tables also illustrate the sampling estimates and the magnitude of the book material actually moved.

Specimen moving contracts

Pertinent excerpts from two moving contracts follow. The first is that used in the National Library of Medicine move for the main move. The move of the History of Medicine collection from Cleveland, Ohio to Bethesda, Maryland was covered by a separate contract. The document shown was also used as the "invitation to bid" and following acceptance then constituted the contract. The second move contract is that prepared at UCLA. The text of these two documents is presented here as an aid in the preparation of such documents. It may be desirable to state a designated priority of moving into the statement of what is to be moved, if this is done, care should be given to providing for changing the priority at the option of the library, since the circumstances of moving may change.

Terms and Conditions

1. Scope and Duration of Contract.

The property to be transported under this Invitation is the property of the National Library of Medicine (hereinafter described as NLM) on whose behalf General Services Administration is acting.

The property consists of books, periodicals, microfilms, portraits, manuscripts, data processing machines, office furniture, shelves and shelving, file cabinets, and miscellaneous equipment and supplies.

The property to be moved is located in the National Library of Medicine Bldg., (basement, first, second, third and fourth floors) 7th and Independence Avenue, S.W., Washington, D.C.

The new location of the property will be in the new National Library of Medicine, 8600 Wisconsin Avenue, Bethesda, Maryland.

The move is to commence on April 13, 1962 (8:00 a.m.) and will continue until completed. The total time for the entire move shall not exceed sixty (60) calendar days.

Prospective bidders may inspect the property at the present location and the new location on January 23, 1962, commencing at 9:00 a.m. in room 115, 7th and Independence Avenue, S.W. Washington, D.C.

2. Services to be Furnished.

a. By Contractor: The contractor shall perform all the services and furnish all equipment, personnel and supplies required to move the property from its present location, transport it to the new location and place the property pursuant to the direction of NLM personnel and/or the Contracting Officer.

Existing bracket type bookstacks now in place at the NLM, 7th & Independence Avenue, S.W., will be emptied of books, dismantled transported to the new building at Bethesda, Maryland, and re-erected where shown in Drawing F-101 (copy attached). The contractor shall supply all labor, materials, tools, appliances and transportation required for this operation, and shall provide any minor parts, such as fasteners, required to erect the bookstacks in the new location.

The stacks to be moved include 862 double and 118 single compartments each having a base shelf and 6 or 7 adjustable shelves. Twenty-one double compartments shall be formed from the singles to make up the 883 double compartments shown on Drawing F-101, "C" Level. Remaining parts shall be stored where directed by NLM personnel and/or the Contracting Officer.

The stacks shall be repaired and have the paint finish touched up as necessary to put them in the same condition of appearance and use they were in before removal to the new location.

Book materials shall be loaded on booktrucks, furnished by NLM or packed in containers (primarily non-book library materials unsuitable for conveyance by booktrucks) by the contractor under the direction of NLM staff members; the loaded booktrucks shall be moved from the stack area onto the moving vans by the contractor, delivered to the new location and the books shelved by contractor under the direction of NLM staff members.

Empty booktrucks shall be returned from the new building to the point of origin by the contractor.

Books will be cleaned by air blast (30 lbs. pressure) by the contractor while booktrucks are on the loading platform prior to placement in moving vans.

NLM staff members will provide direction and guidance relating to the loading of booktrucks and packing of containers and their unloading and unpacking in the new building.

3. Elements of Determining Cost.

Bid shall be submitted on the basis of an overall cost for the entire operation. The charge shall cover all the services, equipment, supplies and containers to be furnished by the contractor to effectuate the handling and movement of the property pursuant to the terms and conditions set forth in this Invitation.

4. Protection of Property:
a. If due to the fault, neglect or dishonesty of the contractor, his agents or employees, any Government-owned or Government-controlled property is lost or damaged during the performance of these requirements, the contractor shall be responsible to the Government for such loss or damage, and the Government, at its option, may, in lieu of payment therefore, require the contractor to replace at his own expense, all property lost or damaged.

b. The contractor shall protect material in his custody against transportation and weather hazards.

5. Damage and Injury:

The contractor assumes responsibility for all damage or injury to persons or property, including the buildings from which removed and to which moved, occassioned through the use and operation of vehicles by its employees and agents, and the contractor, at its own expense, shall maintain adequate public liability and property damage insurance during the continuance of this contract, insuring itself against claims for injury or damage; also workmen's compensation and other legally required insurance with respect to its own employees and agents. The Government shall in no event be liable or responsible for damage or injury to any person or property occassioned through the use or operation of any vehicle by, or the action of, the contractor, its employees and agents, in performing under this contract.

6. Rates and Charges.

For movement of books, furniture, equipment and supplies of the NLM from 7th & Independence Ave., S.W., Washington, D.C., to the new building on the grounds of the National Institutes of Health, Bethesda, Maryland, in accordance with the specifications contained in this Invitation:

Bid Price$ _____

7, Exclusive Use of Contract and Quantity of Services Not Guaranteed.

The Government makes no guarantee or warranty, expressed or implied, as to the exclusive use of this contract, the volume or quantity of material to be serviced, or the type or sufficiency of the equipment that may be required of the contractor to perform the services under this contract.

8. Contract Not Affected by Oral Agreement.

No oral statement of any person shall modify or otherwise affect the terms, conditions or specifications herein stated. All modifications to the contract must be made in writing by the Government Contracting Officer.

9. Permits and Licenses.

The contractor, at his own expense, will obtain and maintain the necessary permits, franchises, licenses and other authorities required for lawfully effecting the movements, handling, and other services to be performed under this contract.

10. Insurance.

The contractor shall furnish to the General Services Administration, within five (5) days subsequent to the date of notice of contract award, a certificate or certificates of insurance, satisfactory to it, in a minimum amount of $100,000 and $300,000 for bodily injury liability and $10,000 for property damage for automobile liability, and a minimum of $25,000 for cargo insurance to cover each transportation vehicle used in the performance of service under this contract.

11. Performance Bond.

A Performance Bond will be required in an amount equal to one hundred (100) percent of the bid of the successful bidder. The surety on the bond may be by any corporation authorized by the Secretary of the Treasury to act as Surety. Standard Form 25 (Performance Bond) will be furnished to the successful bidder with the Notice of Award. The successful bidder will be required to furnish the Performance Bond, properly executed, within two days from the date of the Notice of Award.

12. Default.

Article 11(b) of Standard Form 32, General Provisions, is amended to read as follows:

> "In the event the Government terminates this contract in whole or in part as provided in paragraph (a) of this clause, the Government may procure upon such terms and in such manner as the Contracting Officer may deem appropriate, supplies or services similar to those so terminated, and the Contractor and his Sureties shall be liable to the Government for any excess costs for such similar supplies and services; PROVIDED that the contractor shall continue the performance of this contract to the extent not terminated under the provisions of this clause."

13. Liquidated Damages.

Article 11(f) of Standard Form 32, General Provisions (Supply Contract) is redesignated as Article 11(g) and the following is inserted as Article 11(f):

> "In the event the Government exercises its right of termination as provided in paragraph (a) above, the contractor shall be liable to the Government for excess costs as provided in paragraph (b) above, and in addition, for liquidated damages, in the amount set forth elsewhere in this contract, as fixed, agreed and liquidated damages for each calendar day of delay, until such time as the Government may reasonably obtain delivery or performance of similar supplies or services.
>
> If the contract is not so terminated, notwithstanding delay as provided in paragraph (a) above, the contractor shall continue performance and be liable to the Government for such liquidated damages for each calendar day of delay until the supplies are delivered or the services performed.
>
> The contractor shall not be liable for liquidated damages for delays due to causes which would relieve him from liability for excess costs as provided in paragraph (c) of this clause."

In lieu of the actual damage, the contractor shall pay to the Government, as fixed, agreed and liquidated damage, the sum of $500.00 for each calendar day (fractions prorated) of delay in completing the services required for this move.

14. Nondiscrimination in Employment.

Article 18 of Standard Form 32, General Provisions, is deleted and GSA Form 1714 is substituted herefor . GSA Form 1714 is attached and made a part hereof.

15. Supplemental Provisions.

GSA Form 1424 is incorporated and made a part of this Invitation by attachment hereto.

16. Familiarization With Conditions.

The contractor shall acquaint himself with all available information regarding difficulties which may be encountered and the conditions under which the work must be performed under this contract. The contractor will not be relieved from assuming all responsibility for properly estimating the difficulties and the cost of performing the services required herein because of his failure to investigate the conditions or to become acquainted with all information concerning the service to be performed.

Inventory A
(This is an estimated inventory and the accuracy of the number of pieces of each item cannot be guaranteed).

Books and Periodicals

Approximately 12,000 lin. ft.* of books and periodicals to be designated by NLM personnel.

This collection consists of 1946 serials (W1) located in Main, M1, M2, B14, Russian and Japanese serials (W1) located in B8 and Balcony, and Congresses (W3) located in B7.

Furniture and Equipment

(A) Reference Services Division (1st and 2nd Floor)

Chair, straight, w/arms	10
Desk, Conference type, Steel	1
Credenza Unit, steel 66" long	1
Tray, wood w/casters	1
**Camera, Microfile Recordak Model D	9
Readers, Microfilm	6
Rack, clothing	4
Tables, Office, Steel	7
Typewriters and calculators	8
Stands, Typewriter	2
Cabinet, steel, upright	2
Cabinet, storage, steel	2
Enlarger, photographic	2
Tanks, storage and mixing	2
Hydromixer, Pako	2
Bookcase sections, including base & top	3
**Machine, Xerox, copyflo, Model 1	1
Camera, Copy, Princeton	1
**Machine, Office Copier, Xerox 914	1
Miscellaneous items as directed	

*Linear Feet refers to the measurement of books as arranged on shelf, without gaps, e.g., one shelf of books closely packed equals 3 linear feet.

**To be serviced by factory representative.

(b) Bibliographic Services Division (3rd Floor)

**Camera, Listamatic, Recordak	1
Desk, steel for use with Justowriters	14
Stands, Steel for use with Flexowriters	5
**Machines, Flexiwriters	2
**Machines, Justowriters	16
**Machine, Copying, Xerox 914	1
**Machine, sorting, IBM	1
**Machine, Collator, IBM	1
**Machine, Card Punch, IBM 026	2
Cabinet, IBM Card, 10 drawers	40
Typewriters, manual and electric	20
Chairs, typist	5
Chairs, rotary w/arms	7
Trays, sorting w/casters	7
Rack, tabulating card	2
Cabinet, visible record	4
Cabinet, storage steel	2
Stands, visible record cabinet	2
Cabinets, card, w/contents	3
Tables steel 18x60	7
Table, layout	1
Desk, steel, 30x40	4
Miscellaneous items as directed.	

** To be serviced by factory representatives.

(c) Technical Services Division (2nd Floor)

Cabinet, Card size, wood 60 drawers	33
Tray, sorting, Metal w/casters	15
Typewriters	45
Cabinet, Kardex, Visible record	18
Cabinet, storage	6
File, Open shelf	8
File, Trans-dex	2
Stand, revolving for Kardex	6
Stand, typewriter, metal	4
Map and plan cases	2
Trays w/cards (3x5)	400
Miscellaneous items as directed.	

Books and Periodicals

Approximately 2,500 lin. ft. of books and periodicals to be designated by NLM personnel.

This collection consists of reference volumes located in Reading Room, unbound issues of periodicals ("Current List" section) in Reading Room, the "Z" collection located in the Annex, and Bio-Bibliography collection located in TSD and Room B11.

Books and Periodicals

Approximately 9,000 lin. ft. of books to be designated by NLM personnel. This collection consists of the 20th Century monographs located in Room 119.

Furniture and Equipment

(a) Office of the Director

Bookcase sections	10
Bases, bookcase sections	4
Cabinet, visible file w/stand	2
Cabinets, file, 4 drawer	20
Cabinets, storage, steel	5
Chairs, leg type	130
Chair, rotary w/arms	4
Chair, typist	15
Chalkboard 4x5 w/casters	1
Credenza, steel	3
Desk, conference type	2
Desk, FT, 40x30	12
Rack, clothing	16
Cutter, paper 30"	1
Machine, crosstyping	1
Table, office steel	13
Typewriters and calculators	40

Miscellaneous items as directed.

(b) Reference Services Division (Art Section - Binding Section-
Main Reading Room)

Cabinet, visible record	7
Cabinet, storage	1
Cabinet, filing, 4 drawer	3
Chairs, steel	4
Desk, 60x34	1
Press, book binders	7
Paper, Cutter, heavy duty	1
Table, steel	6
Typewriters	7
Platform truck	2
Truck, book, upright	7
Shelving, steel, X-ray	10 sections
Map and plan cases	4
Cabinet, filing, 4 drawer	16
Case, exhibit	7

Specifications

For

Book and Equipment Move

University Research Library

University of California, Los Angeles, California

Scope and Definition of the Work

1. Scope:

a. The property to be transported under this contract is the property of the University of California and consists of books, periodicals, newspapers, micromaterial, steel shelving, and card catalog trays with cards, card catalog cabinets, microfilm cabinets, contents of desks, file cabinets, typewriters and miscellaneous office furniture and equipment.

b. The property is located on the University of California Campus at 405 Hilgard Avenue, Los Angeles, in the following locations:

(1) Main Library Building, hereinafter referred to as "MLB".

(2) Institute of Industrial relations Library, 2nd Floor, Business Administration Library, Graduate School of Business Administration Building, hereinafter referred to as "IIR."

c. The property in the above locations is to be moved to the following locations:

(1) University Research Library, hereinafter referred to as "URL."

(2) To and within the Main Library Building, hereinafter referred to as "MLB."

2. Definition of Work Scope and Terminology:

Unless otherwise specified, the following requirements, conditions, instructions and definitions shall prevail:

a. The Contractor shall move all books, periodicals, and newspapers on standard size library book trucks, to be supplied by the UCLA Library and/or wooden boxes to be supplied by the the Contractor of a size, shape and construction subject to the approval of the Owner. Book trucks and/or approved wooden

212

boxes shall be used for movement of these materials within and between the buildings concerned. 200 book trucks will be supplied by the University for the use of the contractor.

b. A standard 3-shelf library book truck will hold approximately 9 linear feet of books and periodicals. Each truck shall be loaded so that each of the three shelves contains one (1) row only of books. This is stipulated as maximum load per book truck.

c. The term Linear Feet refers to the measurement of books as arranged on shelf, without gaps, e.g., one shelf of books closely packed equals 3 linear feet.

d. The term "Move" shall have the following meaning: The Contractor shall remove all books, periodicals and newspapers from their present shelves in existing order from left to right, shall place them on book trucks, shall move them to the new designated locations, and shall reshelve them in the same order as directed by UCLA Library Staff at predetermined locations on the shelves as indicated by UCLA Library Staff.

e. Microfilm and microcard materials which are housed in existing microcard and microfilm cabinets shall be moved by the Contractor in the cabinets in which they are presently housed, unless otherwise specified.

f. Catalog cards shall be moved by the Contractor in the trays in which they are housed. The trays shall be placed by the Contractor in boxes furnished by the UCLA Library.

g. Steel Shelving specified to be moved shall be removed by the Contractor from existing shelf columns at their present locations and reinstalled by the Contractor on existing shelf columns at the new locations.

h. The UCLA Library will prepare and provide in advance such labels and directions at all sources and destinations of materials and for use on book trucks, so as to insure the proper movement and location of materials.

i. All loading, movement, and reshelving of books, periodicals and newspapers; all packing, movement and relocation of non-book materials; all movement and relocation of furniture, equipment and desk contents; and all movement of shelving shall be performed by the Contractor under the direction and with the guidance of UCLA Library staff members.

j. The Contractor shall furnish vacuum cleaner equipment to clean all books which are being moved between building while book trucks and/or wooden boxes are on the loading platform or similar location prior to entry into

University Research Library Building. Books being moved within Main Library Building shall be cleaned by vacuum cleaner while on book trucks prior to movement to new locations. Empty shelves in the Main Library Building shall be vacuumed prior to the placement of books and/or material thereon.

k. Movable steel shelves in URL bookstocks have been pre-adjusted to allow 12 inches of clear space between shelves; it is estimated that no more than 850 shelves (out of some 43,000) will require adjustment (i.e., withdrawal of shelf and re-placement at higher point on upright) on direction of UCLA Library Staff members. Contractor shall make such adjustment on direction of UCLA Library Staff.

Section III

Inventory of Material

Inventory A--Books and Periodicals

(This is an estimated inventory and the accuracy of the number of pieces of each item cannot be guaranteed).

(Items listed in descending order of priority)

1. Approximately 57,349 linear feet of books (Central Research Collection) from Stack Levels 1-5 MLB, to Stack Floors 2-5 URL. (Note: This move will continue through entire 60-day period.)

2. Approximately 108 linear feet of large folio atlas volumes from Stack Level 7 MLB, to Locked Cage, 2nd Floor, URL.

3. Approximately 522 linear feet of books from Locked Cage, Stack Level 5 MLB, to Locked Cage, Stack Floor 2, URL.

4. Approximately 1,092 linear feet of books and unbound periodicals from Bindery Preparations Section, Room 20 MLB, to Ground Floor URL.

5. Approximately 1,890 linear feet of books from Acquisitions Department, Room 132 MLB, to Ground Floor URL.

Inventory B--Furniture and Equipment

(This is an estimated inventory and the accuracy of the number of pieces of each item cannot be guaranteed)

(Listed in descending order of priority.)

1. Bindery Preparation Section (MLB, Room 20 to URL A1569, A1574)

Item	Quantity
Adding Machine	1
Foot Stapler	2
Typewriters	4
Letter and Legal File Cabinets	2
(return empties to M. L. B.)	
Visible Files -- Kardex	22
Book Press	4
Paper Cutter	4

Item	Quantity
Bindery Boxes	41
Case, Card Catalog, 18-tray	1
Book Trucks	8
Supply Cabinets - Contents of pam binders and miscellaneous supplies	11
Boxes of Pamphlet binders	15
Staff desk contents	3

2. Acquisitions Department (MLB, Room 132 to URL A1540, 1540E-J)

Item	Quantity
Typewriter	31
Microfilm reader, Kodagraph	1
Microfilm Camera	1
Flexowriter	1
Flexowriter tape holder	1
Western Union Desk Fax (To be serviced by company representative)	1
Xerox Winding Machine	1
6-drawer card file, wood	1
Calculator	1
Adding Machines	2
Paper cutters	2
Case, card catalog, 60-tray, blond wood, 14-1/2" x 17"	1
Caddy-files (Return empties to MLB)	9
2-drawer card file, steel	4
2-drawer card file, wood	3
6-drawer card file, wood	1
Microfilm Winder	1
Book Trucks	16
Supply Cabinets (Contents only)	2
File Cabinets (return empties to M.L.B.)	14
Staff Desk Contents	55

3. Bibliographers (MLB, Rooms 90, 390B to URL Room 1540A-D)

Item	Quantity
Typewriters	8
Desk contents	6
4-drawer file, letter size, metal (return empties to MLB)	2
5-drawer file, letter size, metal (return empties to MLB)	2

Index

218